Aphorisms

On

the New Testament Offices

and their

Relationship to the Congregation

On the Question of the Church's Polity[1]

By

Wilhelm Löhe
Lutheran Pastor
Nuremberg

Publishing House of the Joh. Phil. Raw Bookstore
1849

translated by Dr. John R. Stephenson

Repristination Press
Malone, Texas

© 2008 by John R. Stephenson.
All rights reserved by Repristination Press.

Repristination Press
P.O. Box 173 Bynum, Texas 76631
www.repristination press.com

Hardcover Edition—May 2008

Paperback Edition—September 2013
ISBN 1-891469-37-1

Table of Contents

Table of Contents 3
Translator's Preface 5
Foreword 11
I. Concerning the Congregation 13
II. Jewish Christians and Gentile Christians 17
III. On the Holy Office in General 21
IV. The Apostles 27
V. On the Prophets of the New Testament 39
VI. The Evangelists 45
    Ac 8:12 ff in connection with 21:8 .... *45*
    2 Tim 4:5 .... *46*
VII. Presbyters and Bishops 53
VIII. The Deacons 75
IX. Concerning Ordination 72
X. Remark on Teaching and Preaching without Ordination 101
XI. The First Synod at Jerusalem 105
XII. Application of the Foregoing to the Present Circumstances . 111
Editorial Endnotes 126

Translator's Preface

A word of explanation is in order concerning how I came, several years ago, to set myself to rendering into English the two works that his sometime fellow worker and later chief (and still unsurpassed) biographer, Johannes Deinzer, considered Wilhelm Löhe's "most significant theological achievement" (D III:76).

Almost three decades past, John Kleinig, then studying at Cambridge, England, introduced Löhe to my field of vision and infected me with some of his own love and admiration for this major Lutheran Father of the 19th century. Spurred by John's recommendation, my chancing upon an original edition of the *Aphorismen über die neutestamentlichen Ämter* of 1849 in the library of Westfield House led to my spending some evenings reading them with interest before turning to other more urgent tasks.

Precisely twenty years ago, during my first weeks at the St Catharines seminary, Mrs Norma Merklinger, widow of a well known Canadian Lutheran military chaplain from the era of the Second World War, made me the generous personal gift of her late husband's three-volume set of Johannes Deinzer's classic Löhe biography[2] (cited as D followed by the relevant volume and page number). As time went on, I dipped occasionally into Deinzer's narrative and studied a goodly portion of the third volume in preparation for a paper delivered to our East District pastoral conference in the early 1990s as Lutheran Church Canada moved towards the reintroduction of the male and female diaconate, which is now a distinctive feature of our synodical life.

Twiddling my thumbs and craving a new "project" after the completion and publication of my *Confessional Lutheran Dogmatics* monograph on *The Lord's Supper*, I hit upon the idea of translating Löhe's 1849 *Aphorisms*, mainly as a means of discovering for myself what "all the fuss was about" in the controversies over "Church and Office" that raged in the 1840s and 1850s between such protagonists as Grabau, Löhe, and Walther.[3] The translation proceeded much quicker than expected, and before long I began to render into English also the successor volume, the *New Aphorisms* of 1851.

The first draft of my translation was based on the text given in the relevant volume of Löhe's *Gesammelte Werke* (Collected Works), published by Freimund Verlag in Neuendettelsau, Bavaria. It did not occur to me that an original edition of both sets of *Aphorisms* lay but a few inches away from the *Gesammelte Werke* on the shelves of our seminary library: at the time of our founding, we received generous donations of rare books from our mother seminary, then in the process of relocating from Springfield IL to Fort Wayne IN.

I am grateful to the Rt Revd James Heiser for his willingness to include this translation in the publishing schedule of Repristination Press.

Although he was asked, courteously and in his own language, for permission to print an English translation of the text given in *GW* V/1:253-330, the director of Freimund Verlag (publishing house), declined to give his blessing to this project. For more than two years, this negative reaction appeared to preclude Repristination Press's going ahead with the issuance of this translation, but two factors at length appeared to open the door to publication.

First, Pr David Petersen, of Redeemer Lutheran Church, Fort Wayne IN, alerted Bishop Heiser and myself to the likelihood that the Freimund text, published back in 1954, might itself by now be in the public domain.

Second, one day I stumbled across the original editions of both sets of *Aphorisms* that form part of the collection of the St Catharines seminary. These texts, released in Nuremberg more than a century and a half ago by long extinct publishing houses, are most certainly in the public domain!

So I have painstakingly revised my whole translation of these 1849 *Aphorisms* on the basis of the original text, aiming to assist those who might wish to compare my rendering with the original by including the page numbers of the latter in square brackets in the course of the former. Recourse to the original had the advantage that I noticed, more than I had when using the Freimund version, how Löhe expressed emphasis by use of the German convention of *Sperrdruck*/spaced print, which I have rendered through italics. I hope but cannot guarantee that my eyes, no longer young and much dependent on bifocal lenses, have caught every occurrence of this phenomenon. The original edition also contains several misprints corrected in the Freimund version. Again, I hope that I have registered every typographical error and drawn it to the attention of the reader at the appropriate point in the editorial endnotes. I wish that more time had been available to me for diligent checking and revising of my translation, and presume with a mixture of boldness and diffidence to place this effort before the reader in the hope that English-language Löhe studies may benefit hereby.

I thank my good friend John Kleinig for kindly reading through the whole of my first draft, comparing it with the German text, and, while agreeing that I have accurately caught the sense of the original, making many suggestions for improvement, most of which I have incorporated in what follows. As Dr Kleinig has accompanied the Löhe studies he stimulated almost three decades ago, I would emphasise that the text now offered during this bicentennial year of Löhe's birth is my responsibility, not his.

August Vilmar, himself a renowned expert in German literature, praised Löhe as the writer of the most beautiful German since Goethe (D III:334). While I have endeavored to be as faithful as possible to the literarily impressive original, I have presumed for the sake of readers at home in contemporary English to break up not a few of Löhe's over-lengthy sentences into smaller segments and also, from time to time, to replace the passive with the active voice.

All that appears in square brackets is the work of the translator as Löhe's editor and represents either (1) the German original, presented for the benefit of readers familiar with this language or (2) material not present in the original yet useful for its explication or (3) an indication of the English Bible version used (mainly the Revised Standard Version) when I have not offered my own rendition of the Luther Bible. We have decided to retain Löhe's copious (intentionally parenthetical) references to the Greek text of the New Testament. Although he maintained that readers without Greek could read around these references, by the end of his section on the diaconate Löhe is beginning to argue straight from the original language. Once he embarks on the 35th aphorism, Löhe's use of Greek is more appropriate to a learned journal than to a work aimed at a popular, albeit educated readership.

Every occurrence of "congregation" in the translation indicates the presence of *Gemeinde* in the original. Where either I or the English Bible translation quoted have followed English convention by rendering Löhe's occasional ἐκκλησία-based *Gemeinde* or *Gemeine* with "church," the German original is immediately noted in square brackets. And while I have translated *Presbyterat* with "presbyterate," I have englished the related term *Presbyterium* with "presbytery."

The original text includes a mere seventeen footnotes, marked by an asterisk at the bottom of the page or a double asterisk when (as rarely occurs) two footnotes appear on the same page. I have numbered these footnotes using lower case Roman numerals. At the end of the translation appear some explanatory editorial endnotes marked in the text by Arabic numerals.

I hope in due course to revise, again on the basis of the original text, my hasty translation of the *New Aphorisms: Church and Office* of 1851, and thank Bishop Heiser for his intention to issue it also under the auspices of Repristination Press.

In preparation for teaching an elective course to mark this Löhe year I have by now read and distilled (for the benefit of my students) most of Deinzer's three-volume biography of his mentor. Those who engage in specialist Löhe studies are well advised not to make a detour around the wealth of personal information so beautifully and skilfully marshalled by Deinzer. Careful attention to his narrative demonstrates that both sets of *Aphorisms* are not to be seen in isolation, but rather in intimate connection with the "churchly program" (D II:273) that Löhe developed with great energy (yet without detriment to his parish duties) in the years when he was most crippled with devastating grief over his wife's early death. The political crisis of 1848 awoke unfounded hopes in Löhe's breast that his "churchly program" might in fact be realised sooner rather than later. In the end of the day, perhaps only half of Löhe's aspirations turned into hard fact, namely, the establishment of the order of deaconesses and the erection of the "caritative" institutions bound up with the "procession of *diakonia* from the altar." To this day much of Lutheranism in the old world remains under the shackles of the State control that Löhe lamented in the shape of the "supreme episcopate of the princes." Moreover, his hopes of a renewed Lutheranism, centred in the sacrament of the altar, gladly and unforcedly practicing "unmixed eucharistic fellowship" (his term for our "closed communion"), and moving toward a greater fullness of liturgy, polity, and life than was achieved in the 16th century, have been sadly disappointed. Both sets of *Aphorisms* emerge from this context of conflict and expectation. With one foot in both Lutheran Orthodoxy and Lutheran Pietism (he would not see these successive ecclesial phenomena as alternatives), Löhe reached back behind these powerful factors in his formation to the New Testament text, his prime motivation being loyalty to revealed truth. From the communion of saints he surely bids us test his assertions against the yardstick of the inspired text.

I thank my technically gifted colleague, Dr Thomas M. Winger, academic dean at the St Catharines seminary, for the kind assistance and patient encouragement whereby he has enabled me to present Repristination Press with a camera-ready document.

As we, now launched into the orbit of middle life, celebrate our silver wedding anniversary on 26 February of this year (five days after the two hundredth anniversary of Löhe's birth), with love and gratitude I dedicate this translation to my wife, Bonnie (née Zimmerman), who, herself a consecrated and active deaconess, is one of Löhe's many spiritual daughters.

John R. Stephenson
St Catharines, Ontario
Shrove Tuesday 2008

[iii]

Foreword

Some years ago I[4] was struck by the customary habit of thoughtlessly reading straight past a mountain of evidence in the Acts of the Apostles and the Epistles on the organic nature and polity of congregations. I therefore sketched out a pattern using headings taken from the origin of the Church[5] and added only a little to it. Into this pattern I gathered the various New Testament passages of the sort already named, and a comprehensive overview of the listed passages made a great impression on me. In particular I was struck by the significance and importance of the holy office for the Church and her governance. At the beginning of the year [iv] 1848 the convictions thus gained became even more important for me through the great events of that time. I was led to develop the single parts of my pattern in aphoristic form and to share them with good friends. This is how the first eleven chapters of these aphorisms arose, which, at the urging of some friends, I now publish along with an addendum in the shape of chapter 12. This is also how the three chapters on Discipline, Fellowship, and Sacrifice took shape that are to be found under the comprehensive title "Draft of a Catechism of Apostolic Life" in the *Proposal for an Association of Lutheran Christians for Apostolic Life* printed at the end of 1848.

I make no claim to present a learned and scholarly work. As a parish pastor writing for parish pastors I have set down in simple form what I have observed in Scripture. The Bible passages are printed together with the Greek text both in order to spare readers the trouble of looking them up and also because the Greek text has an original, convincing quality that is lacking in translation. Those [v] not sufficiently competent in Greek to understand the original will, however, be able to read past these passages without encountering any obstacle to understanding.

12

Certainly, only a few will be pleased with what I have written. There have always been men from whose mouth or pen people have disliked the truth that they would have received gladly from other sources. The results of these aphorisms will perhaps be reproached as *impractical*. Yet there can be very different opinions about what is actually practical. Something can be in use and yet not practical, and something that is not in use and decried as impractical can nevertheless be practical. It not infrequently happens that someone transfers obstacles within himself to outward things and conditions in order to excuse himself before himself. This consideration affords me comfort should anyone wish to invest the results of this little writing with the name "subjective," or, to the extent that they seek after realization, with the description "contrived." [vi] Many label subjective what they do not yet grasp, and contrived what they dislike. People gladly brand the opinion of all or many as objective, whereas the lonely truth must be subjective. What is produced from one's own resources is customarily not labeled contrived, and rightly so; yet it is completely wrong to label as contrived what happens in obedience to divine commandments, even if it occurs at first only among a few. The catchphrases of the day can frighten and deceive many. In the end what is true remains true. May God bless for the reader what is true in these pages! And may what is wrong in them perish by the light of His Holy Spirit! May help come from Him for all of us according to His holy will, and may the praise of His name grow among us amid the world's universal cry of distress and affliction! Amen.

[1]

I. Concerning the Congregation

§1. Those who came to faith in the Lord Jesus were named *disciples* (Ac 6:2; 9:10, 25, 26, 36; 13:52; 14:20, 22, 28), as they had already been named during the time of our Lord's earthly life.

In relation to the apostles their name was *"their people"* (Ac 4:23, the apostles "went back to their own people" [NIV]) or *"brothers"* (Ac 11:1, "apostles and brothers"; 15:3; 16:40; 28:14, 15).

With respect to their calling, their name, beginning at Ac 9:41 and then in other passages (e.g., Rom 1:7), was *"saints."*

At Ac 11:26 they are named *"Christians."*

A beautiful sequence of names: *disciples, brothers, saints, Christians.*

§2. *"The whole multitude of disciples"* (Ac 6:2, 5) that joined together in a single whole at Jerusalem is named *congregation or church* (ἐκκλησία, [Ac] 2:47), the congregation or church that was in Jerusalem (ἡ ἐκκλησία η ἐν Ἱεροσολύμοις, [Ac] 8:1; 11:22). Holy Scripture thus names even a local congregation with the holy name ἐκκλησία, church, congregation. If solely the congregation of Jerusalem were so named, it might perhaps be thought [2] that it only bears the name because to begin with all members of the congregation of Jesus on earth were located in Jerusalem, since initially the small congregation of Jerusalem was the entire Church. Yet this is not the case. The congregation at *Antioch* in Syria also has this name ([Ac] 13:1, "Now in the church [*Gemeinde*] at Antioch– ἐν Ἀντιοχείᾳ κατὰ τὴν οὖσαν ἐκκλησίαν – there were prophets and teachers" [RSV]. [Ac] 14:27, "And when they arrived, they gathered the church [*Gemeinde*] together" [RSV], παραγενόμενοι καὶ συναγαγόντες τὴν ἐκκλησίαν). 1 Cor 16:19 speaks of a congregation or church (ἐκκλησία) in the house of Aquila and Priscilla. ("Aquila and Priscilla, together with the church [*Gemeinde*] in their house, send you hearty greetings in the Lord" [RSV], σὺν τῇ κατ' οἶκον αὐτῶν ἐκκλησίᾳ).

14

Moreover, there are enough passages from which everyone can fetch the proof for himself that the various local congregations of Jesus in the whole world are fully entitled to the name of honor *ecclesiae*, churches. See Ac 16:5; Rom 16:4, "all the churches [*Gemeinen*] of the Gentiles," πᾶσαι αἱ ἐκκλησίαι τῶν ἐθνῶν; Rom 16:16, "All the churches [*Gemeinen*] of Christ greet you," ἀσπάζονται ὑμᾶς αἱ ἐκκλησίαι πᾶσαι τοῦ Χριστοῦ; 1 Cor 16:19, "The churches [*Gemeinen*] of Asia send greetings," ἀσπάζονται ὑμᾶς αἱ ἐκκλησίαι τῆς Ἀσίας. At Rom 16:23– in the passage, "Gaius, who is host to me and to the whole church [*Gemeine*], greets you" [RSV], ἀσπάζεται ὑμᾶς Γάϊος ὁ ξένος μου καὶ τῆς ἐκκλησίας ὅλης–the adjective ὅλη, "whole," firmly combines the members of the congregation in question into a single whole. But we find more than all this in the famous passage Mt 18:15-18. Here *the Lord Himself* dubs a [3] local congregation, a parish, *church (ecclesia)*, at a time when He could only do it in the prophetic Spirit because He did not yet have any local congregations. If anyone wanted to find in the words "Tell it to the church [*Gemeinde*]" a reference to a Jewish congregation, he could easily disprove this notion, because at that time there was still no Jewish congregation that lived in obedience to Jesus. So the Lord looks into the future, congregations everywhere arise before His eye, the earth becomes full of His flocks, He calls them *ecclesiae*, churches, and gives them in Mt 18:15 ff. an inviolable law of the kingdom. He calls what does not exist with such sure Spirit that it will come into being, that He already gives an organic law of life to what does not exist but will do so.

The Independents[6] like to invoke the acknowledgment that the ("independent") local congregation so often bears the name church in the New Testament. They do this in order to confer as many rights as possible on the independent congregation. While they certainly go too far in this, it is nevertheless plain that the Lord and His apostles ascribe many more rights to the individual congregation than we customarily assume. An unprejudiced examination of Mt 18:15-18 shows, for example, that we ascribe to territorial churches [*Landesgemeinden*] and their directorates [*Vorstände*] the right of excommunication that is quite plainly promised to the local congregation and that also belongs to her alone. What advantage do territorial churches and their directorates, bound as these are to one location, have over local congregations and their elders where the internal conditions of a congregation have to be adjudged? We [4] see that even the Independents are, if not mainly, yet partly right.

§3. In a gathering of friends[7] someone maintained that proceeding from the individual to the whole is not the Church's way of being built. He said this against another's[8] assertion that regenerating the Church must begin with forming individual Christian congregations before being able to establish from congregations a great whole that would be worthy of the name Church. It will not be difficult to establish which of the two has the truth on his side. It is certainly true that the Church is not only a collec*tion* but also a collec*tor*[9] of saints; her task in time is not only individual perfection but also, as certainly as love is her life, ingathering of lost sheep, influencing of those who resist, education of the whole human race to eternal life and an assembly of saved and sanctified beings. Yet she cannot be a collec*tor* until she herself is collec*ted* and a collec*tion*. Why is her external effectiveness so slight except for the reason that she herself is fragmented, secularized, inconstant in word and deed? Not until what belongs together is gathered in her and, instead of an aggregate of detached members, a tightly-knit host steps onto the battlefield of time, will paganism and the darkness inside and outside her be overcome and enlightened or else isolated and rendered harmless. Individuals must come together in heaps or congregations and congregations into a whole. If temporal interests and false love did not blind us, we would see the obvious. [5] Not only at the beginning, but also later on, at the time of the Reformation and always, the way of the Church was to build houses from stones and from congregation*s* a single great Congregation of the Lord. As a living stone of the great house of God the individual congregation bears the name of the wide, great, divinely willed whole, the name *ecclesia*, Church. Simply read how in the Acts of the Apostles stone is joined to stone, the Church of Samaria to that of Jerusalem and so forth continually (see the next chapter). We can spare ourselves the effort of supplying proof, since we count on readers who search the Scriptures. A simple reading of the Acts of the Apostles can convince such people of what we have expressed here.

§4. The Acts of the Apostles indeed uses the name *ecclesia* initially only of local congregations. Even the passage Ac 20:28 (29), which has a somewhat universal ring to it in the words "flock of God" (ποίμνιον θεοῦ), speaks nevertheless only of the congregation in Ephesus. Not until the letters of Paul, the great apostle to the world and to the Gentiles, do we see the clear continuation of that holy doctrine of the Lord Jesus which is set before us in Jn 15-17. What is here pictured in the *image of the Vine* and explained in unspeakably beautiful and profound discourses returns in Paul in the image of the *temple* and the *body* of Christ. The body, as it is joined and knit together by every joint from the Head; the temple, as it is built and raised up to God's glory upon Christ the cornerstone and upon the foundation of the apostles and prophets (see also Rv 21); the one, holy, universal, apostolic [6] Church stands before Paul's eyes in a brilliance that fills with joy and amazement all who think the apostle's thoughts after him as they read his words. Here is a kingdom and a building not of this world, elevated beyond all human conceptions, surely constructed, certain of consummation amid all storms, worthy of our patience, sacrifice, and ardor. We recommend to the *devotion and prayerful consideration* of our readers such passages as Rom 12:4ff.; 1 Cor 10-13; Eph 1:22f.; 2:20-22; 4:4ff.; 5:23ff.; Col. 2:19; 3:11 etc. And we protest against anyone's judging what we say in detachment from the Scripture passages that we adduce.

II. Jewish Christians and Gentile Christians

§5. It is a well-known fact that already in the days of His flesh the Lord spoke of His work of redemption as global in scope, as something that would benefit all people and nations. But His disciples did not understand Him, and even after the outpouring of the Holy Spirit at the feast of Pentecost they were not suddenly divested of all Jewish-particularistic notions. Those present from all regions of the world in Jerusalem at the miracle of Pentecost were *Jews and proselytes.* The first congregation was gathered from them, and hence from the sphere of Judaism, and there was as yet no question of accepting such pagans as had not previously become proselytes. The [7] apostles themselves regarded Judaism as a most necessary gateway for all who wanted to come to Christ.

The Lord granted the apostles special revelations in order to lead them into all truth in this matter. Yet these revelations did not occur until a firm parent congregation had been gained from the Jews. Without seeing further ahead, the holy apostles troubled themselves at first only with spreading the Gospel among the Jews of Jerusalem and its neighborhood. When this goal was reached and Zion was walking in light, the necessary steps were taken in the most marvelous and most divine sequence of events to gather the nations to the light of Zion in which they were to walk. Whoever pays attention to this as he reads the Acts of the Apostles is suffused with a sense of spring and sees how this book enjoys an advantage over all others in Holy Scripture in setting forth the outpouring of the Holy Spirit in ever wider circles.

The storm of persecution that arose in Stephen's time dispersed the congregation. The blossom and scent of first life are carried around into all lands by way of preparation. In Jerusalem the deacon Philip became a spare wheel, because not much serving at table was called for there any longer. He fills Samaria with new life. Saul becomes Paul and in preparation for his great calling he goes into formative, salutary, divinely blessed quietude. In the meantime the eyes of Peter–and in and through him of the other believers from the Jews–were opened to the mystery hidden from the foundation of the world of the salvation of the heathen. In Ac 10:10ff. (cf. his account in [Ac] 11:4ff.) Peter receives the [8] revelation of the abolition of the distinction between clean and unclean animals. At the same time he also receives the revelation of the abolition of the further distinction (pointed to by the first) between heathen and Jews and of their relationship to the kingdom of God. This very clear, detailed, unmistakable revelation renders the abolition of the fence between Jews and heathen exempt from doubt. In vs. 28 and even more in vss. 34ff. and 47 Peter shows that he had completely entered into the truth shown him by the Spirit. The *Gentiles*, that is, Cornelius and his household, "received the Word of God" ([Ac] 11:1), an expression that points to their public conversion.

So vividly does [Ac] 11:1, 2ff. display the stubborn clinging to Judaism of the believers from the circumcision that we see it come to an outright dispute with Peter (διεκρίνοντο πρὸς αὐτὸν). Yet there was now no turning back. [Ac] 11:19ff. records a mighty extension of what Peter had learnt in the story of Cornelius and of what he had brought to recognition in Jerusalem in Ac 11:4ff. What happened in Antioch on a large scale occurred on a small scale in Caesarea. Once more there was a vehement dispute for and against the fence and wall of division (γενομένης οὖν στάσεως καὶ συζητήσεως οὐκ ὀλίγης, [Ac] 15:2ff.). Paul and Barnabas prove themselves as pillars, and the first council of the Church, held in Jerusalem, demonstrates the all-sufficiency of the merit of our Lord Jesus Christ for the salvation of all nations ([Ac] 15:6ff.).

From that point on began the slow death of the tendency to Jewish particularism, which wanted to dam and limit the sea of grace to Old Testament beds and watercourses. [9] Passages such as [Ac] 21:20, along with the occasion of the letter to the Galatians and much else, show quite plainly how at that time many Jews did not submit to the authority of the apostolic council of Jerusalem.

Almost all the letters of St Paul expose to us the apostle's tremendous conflict with the apostles of the "circumcision." Yet the Spirit of the Lord triumphed resplendently and the New Testament's sacred principle of love, Gal. 3:28, "There is neither Jew nor Greek, there is neither slave nor free, there is neither male nor female' for you are all one in Christ Jesus" [RSV]), had free course. 1 Cor 7:17 shows us with what holy patience and indulgence St Paul defended the great chief thesis of his life and activity and how he wanted it to be applied. But the glorious major passages on the incorporation of the Gentiles into the body of Christ that we find in Eph 2:11ff.; 3:5ff.; 3:9 can also give us an idea how his soul burned and must burn to cancel the division that God did not will and to bring about the union of all Jesus' sheep into a single flock and of all members into the body of a single Church. He and St John in Revelation glimpsed most brightly the religion of the Cross to which all nations are to be called. In his time St Paul was slandered as a man who had no love for his people, and yet he it was who as a morning star of Zion lifted up light and sun over all the Gentiles.

Once we see how, in the Acts of the Apostles and the letters of Paul, the *Lord* preaches so beautifully and sweetly in words and work [10] the holy doctrine of the call of all nations and Gentiles to Christ, we cannot grasp how preachers can be embarrassed to preach the holy mission from New Testament texts. St Paul speaks with glowing love of what we call mission. Understanding him ourselves and leading others to understand him will do more to spark mission than all accounts reported and sent to us from the heathen world (for which be praise and thanks to God!) of the conversion of individual souls. Soul by soul and congregation by congregation may people from all nations and tongues and languages be found in the body of Jesus! For this purpose the world still stands! All things serve this purpose according to God's will!

III. On the Holy Office in General

§6. After the persecution that had arisen in Stephen's time we find the scattered believers everywhere full of zeal to spread the word of God. Ac 8:4 [RSV], "Now those who were scattered went about preaching the word". Ac 11:19-21 [RSV], "Now those who were scattered because of the persecution that arose over Stephen traveled as far as Phoenicia and Cyprus and Antioch, speaking the word to none except Jews. But there were some of them, men of Cyprus and Cyrene, who on coming to Antioch spoke to the Greeks also, preaching the Lord Jesus. And the hand of the Lord was with them, and a [11] great number that believed turned to the Lord."[1] We do not find that these men were under obligation to preach by virtue of an office that they bore. We must conclude that what drove them was a great love for the kingdom of God and the salvation of souls, even though at the same time we do not wish to deny that many of them may have found the first prompting toward the labor of love of their preaching in a commission of the apostles or some other circumstance. After all, Stephen and Philip had wrought much blessing through their speeches and sermons, to which their *diaconate by no means* obliged them, and which they discharged either by virtue of an immediate impulse of the Holy Spirit or out of free love. Why should not this same love also propel others toward like well doing! Compare [book three] chapter 37 of Eusebius' *Church History*, which gives such a glorious report of a very similar *labor of love* on the part of many disciples at the beginning of the second century.[10]

§7. Certain as it is from what has been said that love freely engaged in proclamation[11] is well pleasing to the Lord, and manifestly evident as it is from Scripture that a greater measure

---

1   Ac 15:35 says of Paul and Barnabas that they "remained in Antioch, teaching and preaching the word of the Lord, *with many others also*" [RSV].

of active participation in the work of spreading the kingdom of God was permitted in the first age, it is nevertheless beyond all doubt that the Lord Jesus Himself *founded an office of the New Testament.* [12] This office may emphatically not be confused with the universal priesthood of all Christians, which no more quashes the office than the office quashes it. Hardly anything can be less tenable than the claim that the office-bearers of the New Testament have their authority from the congregation. The congregation does not confer her authority on them–where might a passage of the New Testament be found to justify this thesis? On the contrary, the authority of the office derives from Him who has gathered His congregation through His holy office and who has founded the office to beget and rear her. The office does not derive from the congregation, but it is much more correct to say that the congregation derives from the office. A certain preacher employed these words in his address thanking King Ludwig I of Bavaria for his proclamation of March 1848: "I stand before you [plural] in God's name in order to give expression to your thoughts and feelings in a holy place." If anyone (naturally incorrectly!) would wish to expound this sentence as though the speaker meant to say that the holy office is the called interpreter of popular religious sentiment, then this would, from the perspective of the correct view of the office, be an irresponsible conception of the office. This would be tantamount to introducing popular sovereignty into the kingdom of God. And yet in the end of the day one would have to arrive at such a conclusion, if in fact the office comes from the congregation. The office is of the Lord and from the Lord, and, *with respect to their office* the office-bearers are, to speak with the faithful Lutheran [Friedrich] Balduin [1575-1627], *ultra sortem humanam elati*, that is, their office elevates them to a standpoint superior to every other human calling. Without such a lofty standpoint, [13] without confidence of a divine calling, the burden of the office is both too heavy and too light. Anyone who bears the office and does not occupy this standpoint lacks any footing. To us at least it is not comprehensible how anyone can cast suspicion on this age-old understanding of the office, which is to be found also in the Lutheran Church, by charging it with infringing too closely on the fundamental article of justification through faith alone.

§8. After the office has endured for 1800 years it would be a sorry task to *prove* that the Lord Jesus did found an office of the New Testament. In this specific place such an effort would be entirely superfluous, since what we have to say here can be regarded as a single interconnected proof of the proposition. Moreover, the proof is easy enough to supply. A simple reference to clear, unmistakable passages of Holy Scripture suffices, such as to 1 Cor 12:28, "And *God* has appointed in the church [*Gemeine*] first apostles, second prophets, third teachers" [RSV]; to 2 Cor 3:6-11, which speaks so beautifully of an "office of the New Testament, not of the letter, but of the Spirit," which consequently also gives the Spirit (cf Gal 3:2-5); to 2 Cor 5:19-21, which talks of a "word of reconciliation" in closest connection with an "office of reconciliation"; and to 1 Tim 4:16, where office and word, indeed also office-bearer and word appear so fused together that St Paul directs Timothy how he may save himself and his hearers. Someone intent on speaking quite superficially could indeed pipe in that the passages from the letters to the Corinthians talk only of the apostolate. [14] And yet, quite apart from other reasons and passages, such an argument would not achieve the purpose of denying the divine office, since the other offices demonstrably grew from the apostolate as branches from a single trunk. In order to destroy this whole objection, just look at 1 Cor 3:5ff. Here St Paul, the high apostle, places himself in a series with Apollos, who was not an apostle, and names both of them together as "servants and fellow workers of God." Likewise in 1 Cor 4:1 the names of honor "servants of Christ and stewards of the mysteries of God" are given to both Apollos and to the apostles Peter and Paul. No less does 1 Tim 4:6 name Timothy too, although no apostle, a "servant of Jesus Christ." Hence St Paul by no means regarded only the apostles as bearers of the holy office, but rather drew much wider boundaries. Paul articulates his meaning most completely in Eph 4:11ff. The

Christ who has ascended into heaven has, he says (just as Elijah at his assumption threw his mantle back upon Elisha) bequeathed to His own a wealth of holy and salutary offices. "And his gifts were that some should be apostles, some prophets, some evangelists, some pastors and teachers, *that the saints be fitted for the work of the office,* for building up the body of Christ" etc. [RSV, with exception of italics, which render Luther's translation] (Αὐτὸς ἔδωκε τοὺς μὲν, ἀποστόλους, τοὺς δὲ, προφήτας, τοὺς δὲ, εὐαγγελιστάς, τοὺς δὲ, ποιμένας καὶ διδασκάλους, πρὸς τὸν καταρτισμὸν τῶν ἁγίων, εἰς ἔργον διακονίας—that they would become the work of the office— εἰς οἰκοδομὴν τοῦ σώματος τοῦ Χριστοῦ). We here see the office in its various offshoots, [15] in all as gift and institution of Christ, all in close connection with the building of the Church and the preparation of her members, which last, when properly prepared, are named a work of the office. Given such language of Holy Scripture, which names the Father (1 Cor 12:28), the Son (Eph 4:11ff.), and the Holy Spirit (Ac 20:28) as the Founder of the office, it would be hard to see how anyone could deny the high dignity and divine origin of the holy office, if the state of the human heart in general and the spirit of the age in particular did not render it all too easily explicable. It is amazing how Holy Scripture has been read! People sought out the dogmatic and ethical passages as the only points to contemplate, while they read past everything else, in particular the many passages that organize, order, and direct the congregations as such, as though they were not–like the dogmatic and ethical pronouncements–written for our instruction.

We have paid the price of being without any organism that has stood the test of time. This is the penalty of our inattentiveness and unteachability. Why have we overlooked the apostles' practice as though it were not there? This is especially the case with the doctrine of the holy office. The office is itself a topic in dogmatics. Nevertheless, hardly any point in our dogmatics is as undeveloped as this. There are manifest contradictions (see the chapter on ordination[2]), which it appears [16] that no one has hitherto seen the need to resolve. As though Scripture said nothing on this topic,[3] everyone has formed his own view of the office, if he did even that. Most pastors have themselves no conception of their office and hence lack all basis and confidence for their public activity. They exercise their office as though they had no right to do so, fainthearted, intimidated by every Tom, Dick, or Harry. What a wretched pity! If only there were no further price to pay! If only the pastors alone suffered their penalty! But look how this deficit exacts its revenge! Everyone is talking of polity, but no one knows what to do. People want no hierarchy and no democracy in the Church and yet don't know how to avoid the one or the other. Quite simple! Hierarchy [17] here, democracy there! *The holy office* is the mid-point of all polity, and, in order for this to be so, the divinity, the divine institution and origin of the office, must be proved to the people from bright and clear

---

2   Entire long sections of the apostolic letters, which every Christian may indeed refer to himself according to his measure, refer in first place to the office-bearers of the New Testament.

3   I was originally minded to say something about call and ordination either here or at the end of my remarks on the rungs of the office. Yet because what I have to say presupposes acquaintance with the rungs [*Stufen*] of the office, I have resolved to spare it till later. I nevertheless presume to add a couple of remarks here that are best written down in the borderland between the third and fourth chapters. There is in the New Testament an extraordinary office, which is distinct from and entirely independent of all the others and which is given immediately by the Lord: the office of *prophecy*. The other offices divide into two areas: *presbyterate* and *diaconate*. Both come, like two rivers from the same source, from the apostolate that itself, after the splitting off of the diaconate, remains at the peak of the presbyterate and gathers all other offices named in Eph 4:11ff. (with the obvious exception of prophecy!) into the domain of the presbyterate. In everything that follows we do not want to forget the separation into presbyterate and diaconate. [All occurrences of the first person singular in this paragraph are in the third person singular in the original.]

passages of Scripture. If the office is from the congregation, then the congregation can give it its marching orders, which it will not fail to do in times like ours. But if it is from the Lord, then its position, authority, and scope must remain as the Lord gave it, and all believers must submit to His ordinance. In this case we have something solid. If the relationship of the congregation to the holy office is prefigured in Holy Scripture, then everything will *smoothly* fall into place if we but find wisdom, freedom, and courage to obey. For the churches to prosper we *need as much* hierarchy and democracy as was to be found in the church polity of the first congregations according to the apostolic *Word*; no one need fear before the measure of Holy Scripture. And yet we are getting ahead of ourselves. At this juncture we only wanted to say that helplessness in matters of church polity derives in large measure from lack of insight into the divine foundation of the office that engenders and rears the Church.

IV. The Apostles

§9. Those generally reluctant to be convinced that the Lord founded an office for the New Testament must at all events fall silent when they consider [18] the *apostles*, for the three synoptic gospels relate with complete unanimity how Christ found His apostles (Mt 4:18ff.; 9:9; Mk 1:16ff.; 2:14; Lk 4:38; 5:2ff., 27; cf. Jn 1:37ff.) and "ordered" them to the holy office (Mk 3:13ff.). He ordered the Twelve–ἐποίησε δώδεκα–that they should be with Him, that He might send them out to preach, and that they might have authority to heal diseases and to drive out devils. Lk 6:13– When it was day, He called His disciples and chose twelve of them, whom He named apostles and sent to the *Jews* (Mt 10:5ff.; Mk 6:7-13; Lk 9:1ff.[4]). All four evangelists relate their sending to *all nations* (Mt 28:16ff.; Mk 16:14ff.; Lk 24:46ff.; and Jn 20:21ff., unless we must accord a special place to the last-named passage). As an appendix to his gospel, Luke relates in the Acts of the Apostles how, before His ascension, Jesus renewed the call ([Ac] 1:2, 8) of the apostles whom He had chosen ([Ac] 1:2, οὕς ἐξελέξατο).

§10. It is evident from what has been said that the calling of the apostles was different during Jesus' lifetime from what it was after His ascension. So long as He Himself was in this temporal life, He preached only to the Jews, and they followed suit. After His ascension, though, they went out not only to Judea, but also to Samaria and "to the ends of the earth," Ac 1:8. And not only their sphere of activity but also their task became different. To the Jews they preached the "kingdom of God" [19] (ἀπέστειλεν αὐτοὺς κηρύσσειν τὴν βασιλείαν τοῦ θεοῦ, καὶ ἰᾶσθαι τοὺς ἀσθενοῦντος, Lk 9:2), "that [it had] drawn near" (πορευόμενοι κηρύσσετε, λέγοντες ὅτι "ἤγγικεν ἡ βασιλεία τῶν οὐρανῶν, Mt 10:7), and that people should repent (ἐξελθόντες

---

4 Lk 10:1ff.: mission of the *Seventy*.

ἐκήρυξαν ἵνα μετανοῶσιν, Mk 6:12). Conversely, after the ascension of Jesus preaching was essentially a preaching *about Him*. They were to become *His witnesses* (ἔσεσθέ μοι μάρτυρες, Ac 1:8. ὑμεῖς δὲ ἐστε μάρτυρες τούτων, Lk 24:48). "Thus it is written, that the Christ should suffer and on the third day rise from the dead, and that repentance and forgiveness of sins should be preached in his name to all nations" (εἰς πάντα τὰ ἔθνη), Lk 24:46ff. [RSV]. They should go into all the world (εἰς τὸν κόσμον ἅπαντα), preach the Gospel to every creature (Mk 16:15), make all nations and Gentiles His pupils (πορευθέντες μαθητεύσατε πάντα τὰ ἔθνη), baptize them into the name of the Father, Son, and Holy Spirit and initiate them into Jesus' blessed order for life (διδάσκοντες αὐτοὺς τηρεῖν πάντα ὅσα ἐνετειλάμην ὑμῖν), Mt 28:19. Thus they should preach and bring forgiveness of sins, life, and salvation to the believers and baptized and damnation to those who obstinately resist (Mk 16:16; Jn 20:22, 23). This was their task and for this purpose extraordinary gifts of the Holy Spirit and great miracles were given them. Peter understood this his calling quite well already before the outpouring of the Holy Spirit, and his overall behavior between Ascension and Pentecost deserves all admiration on account of its great illumination and its conception of the apostolic office. [20] Since a new apostle is to be elected, Peter says that the one to be elected must become, along with the other apostles, a *witness to the resurrection of Jesus* (μάρτυρα τῆς ἀναστάσεως αὐτοῦ, Ac 1:22). On the day of Pentecost the same high apostle describes their life's task, their job description, entirely in these terms. "This Jesus God raised up, and of that we are all witnesses" (τοῦτον τὸν Ἰησοῦν ἀνέστησεν ὁ θεός, οὗ πάντες ἡμεῖς ἐσμεν μάρτυρες), Ac 2:32 [RSV]. The resurrection of Jesus is the focal point of His glorification and of His work, the "seal of the New Testament." The preaching of the Resurrection is accordingly the focal point of all preaching that may rightly be called evangelical. The whole work of Jesus and faith in Him are in vain without the Resurrection. In the Resurrection lies the whole guarantee for everything that the Lord accomplished. This accounts for the fact that all sermons of the apostles that we read in *Acts are testimonies of His resurrection and thereby receive their special character*. The passage Ac 13:30-33 affords undeniable proof that also St Paul conceives the apostolic job description entirely in these terms. "But God raised him from the dead; and for many days he appeared to those who came up with him from Galilee to Jerusalem, *who are now his witnesses to the people. And we bring you the good news that what God promised to the fathers, this he has fulfilled to us their children by raising Jesus* ...[RSV]"

§11. Just as assuredly as we have correctly set forth in §10 according to Holy Scripture the task proper to the apostles, [21] equally assuredly no one could or can receive the[12] apostolate other than *either* one who knew Jesus' work and way of life and was His personal disciple by living with Him so long as He was on earth until His ascension *or* one who came by miraculous paths to knowledge of all these facts and acquaintance with the person of Christ. If therefore with their longing and prayer for apostles the Irvingian sect would really desire men utterly equal to the apostles, their demand could only be met by exceptional and miraculous means. Either the old apostles would have to rise from the dead, or St Paul's miraculous fate would have to be fulfilled in them. To rescue the just-named sect's reputation for sanity we must hope that it simply laments the absence and for the Church's well-being wishes for the availability of men who would be similar to the apostles in light, power, and *far-reaching efficacy*. Be that as it will, of this much we are certain: Holy Scripture itself has established the apostles as a special, irrecoverable privilege of the first age.[5] They are the *foundations* of the heavenly city, as Rv 21:14 shows us, and this they remain even if they do not personally return to this poor world prior to the Lord's coming in glory.

Meanwhile we here wish to set forth in express terms the biblical passages that speak of the prerequisites for the apostolic office.

---

5 In place of this we have other privileges, e.g., the testimony of eighteen Christian centuries.

[22] In Jn 15:26-27 the Lord says, "The Spirit of truth who proceeds from the Father, he will bear witness to me; and you also are witnesses, because you have been with me from the beginning [RSV]." The Holy Spirit bore witness through the apostles. Their witness was divine, because the Holy Spirit prompted it. It was also a human witness because they had been with Jesus from the beginning and had been eyewitnesses of His sufferings and of His glorification. Their witness was simultaneously divine and human with emphasis being placed now on this side and now on the other. Precisely this double authority of the apostolic witness causes it to have such a powerful effect on human souls and to strike the spirits of all hearers as so complete. Who could read the glorious passage from the beginning of the first letter of St John (1:1ff), for example, without being at once humanly overjoyed and drawn to his knees by sheer divine power? "That which was from the beginning, which we have heard, which we have seen with our eyes, which we have looked upon and touched with our hands, concerning the word of life. ...that which we have seen and heard we proclaim also to you, so that you may have fellowship with us; and our fellowship is with the Father and with his Son Jesus Christ" [RSV]. (Cf 2 Pet 1:16ff). These sentiments of the holy apostles formulated from the very beginning, even before the first Pentecost, what was required of those who would be or become apostles.

In Ac 1:21f, when another apostle was to be elected in place of Judas Iscariot, St Peter says, after he has stressed the necessity of filling Judas' [23] place, "So one of the men who have accompanied us during all the time that the Lord Jesus went in and out among us, beginning from the baptism of John until the day when he was taken up from us—one of these men must *become with us a witness of his resurrection*" [RSV]. Nothing can be clearer than this passage.

However clear this passage is, the manner of St Paul's election and call as an apostle must be labeled at least as telling if not even more telling. In Rom 1:1 St Paul calls himself "a servant of Jesus

Christ, called to be an apostle" [RSV] and he claims in vs 5 to have received through Christ "grace and apostleship (ἀποστολὴν; cf. Ac 1:25) to bring about the obedience of faith for the sake of his name among all the nations" [RSV]. In a certain sense he makes a distinction between himself and the other apostles and calls them the "superlative apostles" (τοὺς ὑπερλίαν ἀποστόλους; 2 Cor 11:5 [RSV]). And yet again in 2 Cor 12:11 he frankly claims that he is no less than the superlative apostles, even though he is nothing (οὐδὲν ὑστέρησα τῶν ὑπερλίαν ἀποστόλων, εἰ καὶ οὐδέν εἰμι.). How can this claim be justified, since he was never in Jesus' school and, according to all that *we* know, never even saw Him in the body of death? The claim can in fact be fully justified in that he *did*, as the several accounts of his conversion make irrefutably clear, see the Lord in the body of the resurrection. See, e.g., Ac 9:3-8, cf. vs 27. In 1 Cor 15:1ff he lists the various post-Resurrection appearances of Jesus and mentions the last as [24] having occurred to himself with the words, "Last of all, as to one untimely born, he appeared also to me" [RSV] (ἔσχατον δὲ πάντων ὡσπερεὶ τῷ ἐκτρώματι ὤφθη κἀμοί). He thus made the personal acquaintance of the risen Jesus. He did not see Him in a vision, but his bodily eyes saw Him and were struck blind by the brilliance of the glory of the Lord. Besides, among all men he had the distinction of seeing the Lord as an ἐκτρώμα, an untimely birth, i.e., in the unconverted state, for the purpose of his being converted and invested with the apostolic office. Therefore he also cries out in 1 Cor 9:1, "Am I not free? Am I not an apostle? Have I not seen Jesus our Lord?" [RSV] (Οὐκ εἰμὶ ἐλεύθερος; οὐκ εἰμὶ ἀπόστολος; οὐχὶ Ἰησοῦν τὸν Κύριον ἡμῶν ἑώρακα;). Yet Paul not only *saw* the Risen One, not is he only a witness of His resurrection, but he is also Jesus' *personal pupil* just like the other apostles. If he did not live with Him here below, he was caught up to Him into Paradise and the third heaven, where he heard his Lord's words "that cannot be told" [RSV] (ἄρρητα ῥήματα). In 1 Cor 11:23ff. he recounts the institution of the holy office and adds, "For I received from the Lord what I also delivered to you" [RSV]

(Ἐγὼ παρέλαβον ἀπὸ τοῦ κυρίου ὃ καὶ παρέδωκα ὑμῖν). In 1 Cor 15:3 he introduces the brief overview of the life, death, and resurrection of Jesus and the entire discourse on the resurrection with the words, "I delivered to you ...what I also received: [RSV] (παρέδωκα ὑμῖν, ὃ καὶ παρέλαβον). [25] And in Gal 1:11-12 he says, "For I would have you know, brethren, that the gospel preached by me is not man's gospel. For I did not receive it from man, nor was I taught it, but it came through a revelation of Jesus Christ" [RSV] (Γνωρίζω δὲ ὑμῖν, ἀδελφοί, τὸ εὐαγγέλιον τὸ εὐαγγελισθὲν ὑπ' ἐμοῦ, ὅτι οὐκ ἔστι κατὰ ἄνθρωπον. οὐδὲ γὰρ ἐγὼ παρὰ ἀνθρώπου παρέλαβον αὐτό, οὔτε ἐδιδάχθην, ἀλλὰ δι' ἀποκαλύψεως Ἰησοῦ Χριστοῦ). And what he claims in these words he proves in the course of the letter to the Galatians, so that we genuinely find the signs of an apostle in St Paul and can and must fit him in along with the others.

§12. It is a well-known fact that the Lord chose *precisely twelve* apostles and neither more nor less. Equally well known is the interpretation of the number twelve in terms of the twelve tribes of Israel, an interpretation that has sufficient support in Holy Scripture for it to be regarded as completely correct. That the number twelve was important for the Lord as He chose apostles for Himself is also seen from the fact that alongside the apostles He also chose seventy disciples to whom He allotted a similar sphere of duties to the one assigned the apostles (Lk 10:1ff). Why did He not immediately select seventy more emissaries if the Twelve were too few for Him? Because He wanted to choose twelve and, alongside them, seventy, and because this and precisely this demarcation of the number of both the Twelve and the Seventy was important for Him. But if it mattered for the Lord to make His choice in just this way, then it mattered and it matters for us to pay heed to this His choice and numbering. [26] Without going into the interpretation of the number seventy, let us tarry with the apostles' number of twelve and conclude that there had to be twelve apostles. Our conclusion is justified by the mouth of Peter in Ac 1:20, 21. "His episcopate [*Bistum*] let another take"

(Τὴν ἐπισκοπὴν αὐτοῦ λάβοι ἕτερος), specifies the apostle from Ps 109:8 and concludes, "One of these men must become with us a witness to his resurrection" [Ac 1:23 RSV] (δεῖ οὖν ... μάρτυρα τῆς ἀναστάσεως αὐτοῦ γενέσθαι σὺν ἡμῖν ἕνα τούτων). We see how the apostle is pressing to make good the number twelve that had been damaged by Judas' apostasy. For him this number is inviolable, and we see from passages such as the already cited Rv 21:14 that other parts of Holy Scripture likewise regard it as inviolable.

Yet if the number twelve is so inviolable, in what relationship does St Paul then stand to the Twelve? Olshausen is so overcome by this question that he reaches for a remedy of despair: he wants the election of St Matthias to be regarded as hasty and invalid in order to secure for St Paul his seat among the company of the Twelve. This solution offers little help, though, since Ac 14:14 dubs not only Paul but also Barnabas as an apostle, so that there would still be a thirteenth apostle left over. Let us therefore leave everything as it is! Matthias' election is valid, supremely because it is not only human but also–through the casting of a lot–divine (Ac 1:25-26). Moreover, the strict connection between Ac 1:26 and 2:1ff does not [27] permit any other conclusion than that Matthias received the Holy Spirit along with the Eleven, thereby being recognized by the Lord. The Twelve form a closed number, to which even St Paul does not belong. What God has joined together let no man put asunder, and what He has separated let no man will to join. St Paul is an apostle equal in dignity and majesty to the others, but to the number twelve so laden with significance for the twelve tribes of Israel he does not belong. Let this fact stand and become somewhat accustomed to it, and the stature of the solitary great apostle to the Gentiles only rises higher. Indeed, he ought not to stand in such isolation, for Barnabas and his activity do not need to disappear so much before the splendor of Paul as is actually the case. Moreover, still others might stand alongside Paul on the streets of the Gentiles as true apostles in the full sense of the name. Paul would still remain

Paul and the lofty apostle (ὁ ὑπερλίαν ἀπόστολος). While equal in office to all other apostles, he has different connections. Only from this perspective do passages such as Ac 13:31, where Paul distinguishes his and Barnabas' testimony from the eyewitness testimony of the Twelve, acquire their full light. We recognize here not only the most lovable modesty, but also a righteousness that dovetails with the proverb *Qui bene distinguit, bene docet* (Whoever distinguishes well teaches well).

§13. We might surely say much concerning the *gifts* of the Holy Spirit conferred on the holy apostles. Here we should like to take the opportunity of emphasizing only two such phenomena, because, [28] conspicuous as they are, they have given rise to much misinterpretation.

The story of Ananias and Sapphira in Ac 5 and Peter's dealings with Simon, the magician of Samaria, in Ac 8:20ff, prove his having a *superhuman acuteness of spirit and of looking into others' souls*. Although Simon did somewhat wear his heart on his sleeve, nevertheless what Peter said about and to him digs into the depths of a corrupt heart: "Your silver perish with you, because you thought you could obtain the gift of God with money! You have neither part nor lot in this matter, for your heart is not right before God. Repent therefore of this wickedness of yours, and pray to the Lord that, if possible, the intent of your heart may be forgiven you" [Ac 8:20ff., RSV] (Τὸ ἀργύριόν σου σὺν σοὶ εἴη εἰς ἀπώλειαν, ὅτι τὴν δωρεὰν τοῦ Θεοῦ ἐνόμισας διὰ χρημάτων κτᾶσθαι. οὐκ ἔστι σοι μερὶς οὐδὲ κλῆρος ἐν τῷ λόγῳ τούτῳ. ἡ γὰρ καρδία σου οὐκ ἔστιν εὐθεῖα ἐνώπιον τοῦ Θεοῦ. μετανόησον οὖν ἀπὸ τῆς κακίας σου ταύτης, καὶ δεήθητι τοῦ Θεοῦ, εἰ ἄρα ἀφεθήσεταί σοι ἡ ἐπίνοια τῆς καρδίας σου. εἰς γὰρ χολὴν πικρίας καὶ σύνδεσμον ἀδικίας ὁρῶ σε ὄντα.). And these gifts are found in full measure in the story of Sapphira and Ananias! Who had betrayed their hypocrisy to Peter, and by whom was he instructed? And nonetheless he sees through their deceit and uncovers it to the very last detail, whereupon a strict judgment overtakes the hypocrites. We have here a gift of testing and distinguishing spirits that we seek in vain to perceive in other teachers and that no one [29] will pretend to possess. What brought about this acute judgment of others was the life before the face of God that we must ascribe to the apostles, along with extraordinary illumination from above. Not that we wish in any way to claim that this gift of acutely judging human hearts was a possession of the apostles that they used at all times with the same infallibility as was displayed in the two cases mentioned above. It was important at the very outset of the kingdom of God to give telling examples of God's displeasure at hypocrites and impure people. These examples stand at all times without our being obliged to set up extraordinary judgments and an inexorable intervention of God as a canon of divine activity for all times and cases. While we may compare with these instances the story of the magician Elymas in Paphos (Ac 13:6ff), weaknesses of the personal, inner life must have blemished the records of both Paul and Peter, and during such times judgments such as those just listed will hardly have been possible. For fully correct judgment of others involves the heart that is to do the judging's not being beclouded by any passion or dulled by any lukewarmness or weakness.

A second phenomenon that we must briefly touch on is the apostles' gift, mentioned in Ac 8:17, of *communicating the extraordinary gifts of the Holy Spirit through the laying on of their hands*. This gift is highly remarkable precisely with respect to the Samaritans upon whom it was exercised (see 14.b below). The Samaritans had received the ordinary gift of the Holy Spirit through Holy Baptism, which the deacon Philip [30] conferred on them. It goes indeed without saying that this ordinary gift was in no way to be topped up, not even through apostolic hands. Just as, after receiving baptism, the Ethiopian treasurer left his baptizer, the deacon Philip, full of the light and power of the Holy Spirit and nothing further needed to be given him for his salvation, so the Samaritans also had received sufficient for eternal life through Philip's baptism. What the apostles added when they laid on their hands was of importance not for eternal life but for the life and prosperity of the first congregations, to the extent that the extraordinary gifts of the Holy Spirit were noticed in those who had them and were able by their brilliance to lead the hearts of others to Jesus Himself, the source of good gifts. The extraordinary gifts were also independent of baptism, as is shown in Ac 10, where they were given to Cornelius along with his friends before baptism, and yet in such a way that they by no means rendered holy baptism superfluous. In the same story it was finally shown that the Lord did not even bind the gifts named to the hands of the apostles, for He gave them to Cornelius immediately, without apostolic hands, under Peter's preaching. Let us then divide the gifts of miracles and tongues, which the apostles had and conferred, from the better gifts of the Spirit, which are necessary because they have saving power.

§14. Let us be permitted in closing to make some looser remarks on the topic of the *effectiveness* of the apostles.

a. Ever since in my book *On the Church* I [31] dared to express some opinions on the universal call of all peoples already at the time of the apostles and also subsequently which, of great antiquity as they are, have also been acknowledged by those who first believed the Word and then sought the proof, much has been said here and there against these opinions (if I do not somewhat derogate from the truth by so forthrightly labeling them opinions) that has not been able to convince me. On the contrary, in the aftermath I have found God's Word much clearer than previously, and the testimonies of the fathers,[6] with which I have become somewhat more precisely acquainted since then, have given me the proof that I did not write so incorrectly and that what I believed and accordingly expressed did not strike other men, whom all Christians revere for their insight, as mere absurdity and narrow-minded literalism. I might back up what I have advocated, and whether here or in another place I might be tempted to offer

---

6 Precisely *Origen*, whom at least no one will call insipid or ignorant, says much that can hardly be taken otherwise than as a confirmation of what I and others have maintained.

a detailed presentation of the doctrine in question. Yet I have refrained from this temptation to this point, because the topic is poles removed from the issues that are now agitating the Church, and I did not want to encourage the impression that I am riding a hobbyhorse. This is said in passing. What I wanted to emphasize in this place is the following:

b. After Stephen's death arose a great persecution in Jerusalem. The congregation scattered, while [32] the apostles remained in Jerusalem so that the scattered might have a certain refuge. Those who were scattered came to Samaria and preached, and so the deacon Philip preached there with great success. The apostles Peter and John came and confirmed the great work through the extraordinary gifts, and on their way home they themselves preached the Gospel to many Samaritan villages (πολλὰς τε κώμας τῶν Σαμαριτῶν εὐηγγελίζοντο, Ac 8:25). Thus the first believers from the Jews and the apostles had no horror of the Samaritans as they did of the Gentiles, but in this point they completely differed from other Jews! As we register the hatred of the Samaritans that all Jews sucked in with their mothers' milk and the apostles' vigorous dedication to preaching to the Gentiles, an awe-filled reference to the apostles' love of the Samaritans is certainly not out of place. The One who during His days on earth told so gladly of the Good Samaritan and of the Samaritan who gave thanks may in this point have overcome the hearts of His disciples at an early stage and made their hearts similar to His own.

c. This is all that we shall say here on the apostles' effectiveness upon the nascent Samaritan congregations. And now at the end of this chapter simply a couple of extra remarks on the apostles' effectiveness upon congregations already in being. The Lord had commanded His apostles to be concerned that all peoples become Christian, but He had also added to His command to baptize, "Teach them (the baptized peoples) to keep everything that I have commanded you." From this proceeds the corollary that the apostles did not [33] have to pay heed to the peoples only for so long as they were not baptized, but that also the baptized peoples and especially they were commended to their especial care and love. Hence St Paul in 2 Cor 11:28 reckons the care of all the congregations to the obligations of his office‛ (τὴν μέριμναν πασῶν τῶν ἐκκλησιῶν), a care that is also brilliantly in action in all the so-called Catholic Epistles of the apostles, and not only in them, but also in all letters. Yet with this care there was given at the same time to the apostles by the Lord Himself a salutary authority not against but for the congregations and for their blessing. The founders of all the congregations, the commencers of the entire salutary movement, the most faithful friends of all converted souls should keep the leadership as long as they were on earth, and they should receive the respect and veneration of all. Therefore in 1 The 4:8 St Paul desires that he be not despised, lest God be despised thereby. St Peter interprets the lie committed against him by Ananias and Sapphira as a lie against the Holy Spirit, that is, against God, who ruled in and through the apostles (Ac 5:3, 4). St Paul gives commands even to his fellow worker Timothy (ταύτην τὴν παραγγελίαν παρατίθεμαί σοι, 1 Tim 1:18), and in 2 Cor 10:8ff he uses majestic words of the authority that the Lord has given him for building the Church up and not for destroying her (ἐξουσία ἣν ἔδωκεν ὁ κύριος ημιν εἰς οἰκοδομὴν καὶ οὐκ εἰς καθαίρεσιν ὑμῶν). Few hints are given, but whoever would draw from them the decision to consider whether the prestige of the apostles in the first [34] congregations was so great and overwhelming would surely become aware that these men governed in the congregations with a dignity and authority over against which all earthly dignity and majesty stands very much in the shade. Care for all congregations, what a task! Authority over all congregations, what a lofty position! The humble and yet so strong princes of the Church mount ever higher and higher before our eyes, the more we gather and heed what Scripture says of their dignity and burden. The statement that the apostles enjoy a unique and incomparable position in the history of the Church permits no contradiction, whether we consider their gift of their burden and task or their dignity and full authority.

V. On the Prophets of the New Testament

§15. The Old Testament had its prophets. No less do we also find prophets of the New Testament. "Therefore," says Christ in Mt 23:34, "I send you *prophets* and wise men and scribes [RSV]" (ἰδοὺ, ἐγὼ ἀποστέλλω πρὸς ὑμᾶς προφήτας καὶ σοφοὺς καὶ γραμματεῖς). Correspondingly we also find the prophets in second place in the sequence of sacred offices both in 1 Cor 12:28 ("And God has appointed in the church [*Gemeine*] first apostles, second *prophets*" [RSV]) and in Eph 4:11 ("He, Christ, appointed some as apostles and others as *prophets*"). Set over against them in 2 The 2:3, 1 Tim 4:1, [35] and 2 Pet 2:1, as shadowy counterfeits, are deceitful prophetic powers of hell. We also find a rich measure and brilliant display of the prophetic gift in the apostles, who seem to have possessed all glorious gifts needful and beneficial for the foundation and governance of the Church. Yet we also find them in others. In Ac 11:27 we first encounter prophets who came down to Jerusalem from Antioch. Preeminent among them is *Agabus* (cf Ac 21:4ff.), whom some (see Quenstedt in the *Antiquitates*, p. 78) name as one of the seventy disciples. They applied their gift to relieving ahead of time the shortages that would afflict many poor Jewish Christians in a great famine that had been revealed to them. The gift of the Holy Spirit thus served to mitigate the temporal misery of believers, certainly not apart from the special purpose of God, in order to show how much He cares for His own in these things also. The One who dwells in heaven and in the sanctuary also cares about the span of time that is oftentimes so long and hard for weak Christians here below. According to Ac 13:1 there were in Antioch "prophets and teachers" (cf the relationship and juxtaposition to the gifts as set forth in 1 Cor 12:28), and the two gifts were indeed united in the same persons (cf Ac 11:22-26). The names of the Antiochene prophets are: Barnabas, Simeon called Niger, Lucius of Cyrene, Manaen, and Saul, who is named last as though he had not at that time become so remarkable among the others. Vs. 2 attributes a special "serving God" (λειτουργειν τω θεω) to these prophets, a communally exercised [36] prayer and supplication in the course of which they received the divine command to set apart Barnabas and Saul for a special office among the Gentiles. In Ac 15:32 we find Judas Barsabas and Silas not simply as esteemed leaders of the congregation at Antioch (ἄνδρες ἡγούμενοι ἐν τοῖς ἀδελφοῖς, v. 22) but also as *prophets*, in which capacity they admonished the brethren with many words and strengthened them (Ἰούδας τε καὶ Σιλᾶς καὶ αὐτοὶ προφῆται ὄντες διὰ λόγου πολλοῦ παρεκάλεσαν τοὺς ἀδελφοὺς καὶ ἐπεστήριξαν). In Ac 20:23 and 21:4, 9, 10, 11 we find prophets and prophetesses, in particular once more the prophet Agabus, who, like the Old Testament prophets, prophesies at once with words and through signs.

Above all in the Letter to the Ephesians we find much mention of the New Testament prophets. When 2:19-20 says that the Ephesians are "no longer strangers and sojourners, but ...fellow citizens with the saints and members of the household of God, built upon the foundation of the apostles and prophets, Christ Jesus himself being the cornerstone [RSV]," those who are disinclined to look for prophetic gifts in the New Testament can indeed read past this passage and think immediately of Old Testament prophets. Yet to the foundation of which Jesus is the cornerstone and the apostles the first stones the New Testament prophets might, more fittingly, concretely, and correctly, be added as stones of second order that follow the apostles (apostles–and–prophets!). Against this supposition, see Quenstedt, *Antiquitates*, p. 77 §6. After all, no one can deny that the New Testament prophets are named immediately afterwards in 3:5. In the latter [37] passage St Paul speaks of the chief revelation of *his* life, of the mystery that the Gentiles are fellow heirs (vs 6), and says that this mystery was not made known to the children of men in former ages as it is now being revealed to God's holy apostles and prophets through the Spirit. Only New Testament prophets can be meant here.

§16. We might here deal with the distinction between various kinds of prophecy and demonstrate differing degrees of intensity within the prophetic gift. We might seek to harmonize texts such as Ac 21:9 and 1 Cor 14:34. The first of these assures us of the magnificent virgins, the daughters of the evangelist Philip (cf their further fortunes in Eusebius, *History of the Church* 3.31[7]), that, "They prophesied," while the second forbids women in the congregation to prophesy and to speak. Yet our overall task here is not to enter into the details of the gifts of the Holy Spirit in general and of that of prophecy in particular. We intend to do no more than convey something of the often-overlooked organizing and ordering aspect of the apostolic writings and to highlight its importance through its discussion. These pages were written down for this purpose, originally for good friends. But our opinion of the New Testament prophets and their importance is this. Our conviction is not such as to assert a complete cessation of the prophetic gift in every measure and sense. On the contrary, we believe that the Lord never caused this spring of His house to dry up completely. [38] Just as the apostles were men of the first age, designated to become foundation stones of the building whose cornerstone is Jesus Christ, so too the entire activity of those first prophets, who are spoken of in the texts just cited, was geared to the foundation, and first extension, of the Church. The apostles too were prophets, and that to a pre-eminent degree. Just think of St John. And yet the prominent feature of their testimony was its focus on completed deeds of God, on the work and consummation of Jesus, rather than on what was hidden and still future. The opposite was the case with the prophets. While the apostles worked not only to animate and awaken but also to gather, purify, and order, and while they had in mind the edifice of the entire Church and moreover the insertion and growth of individual congregations within the great whole of the Church, the nature of the prophets' activity was more to animate and awaken. The holy apostles aimed above all at the gradual transfiguration and sanctification of mankind.

---

7   The giving of the name *apostle* to the Deacon Philip is an obvious mix-up.

With heavenly power and wisdom they conducted the abundant tributaries of the other world into Jesus' fields and gardens. But the prophets were witnesses and proofs of the Church's immediate contact with the other world. Whenever it emerged their activity was a reminder of the Lord's presence that He had promised to His own, a special sort of reminder of the invisible eternal world which the Church [*Gemeinde*] was called to enter. Just as in the Old Testament the Lord willed to lead the people, by high priest and priests and the whole priestly system, to the peace of a holy existence [39] on earth, so in the New Testament He resolved to do it to all peoples by the apostles and by the total work of the New Testament, which grew out of the fullness of the apostolate. Priesthood in the Old Testament and apostolate and office in the New bring God's order into God's people. In their capacity as God's direct ambassadors, immediately filled and led by Him, prophets in the Old Testament constantly intervened afresh in the Church to keep alive and constantly refresh among the people the true meaning of everything God had instituted, the priesthood, the worship etc. So too the prophets of the New Testament, who were greater in number than the apostles and so able to be more universally present than they, likewise kept on stepping in at first hand to bring the organized congregations that stood under the governance of the apostles into ever new and fresh contact with the fountain of our life. Their activity turned out to be especially refreshing and enlivening for the poor human heart, which so easily becomes worn and weary in everything spiritual. How needful such activity was for the young Church [*Gemeinde*] of Jesus! How powerfully she could be advanced and increased thereby becomes especially evident when the biblical examples adduced above lead us to realize how conspicuously and unmistakably the prophets arose as messengers of the direct care of God and our Savior.

Moreover, what has just been said shows how sad it would be if we were totally bereft of all prophetic gifts. Though we have as little right to crave and desire prophecy in the measure of the first [40] foundational prophets as we have to expect the gifts of office in the measure of the first presbyters, the *apostles*, we still stand, to some extent, in need of prophecy's life-giving refreshment, just as we also stand, to a certain degree, in need of the holy office that leads us in holy order to eternal life. After all, everything mentioned in Rom 12:6ff belongs to the Holy Spirit's extraordinary gifts of grace that are not available to everyone! And yet many of those gifts relate especially to the gift of prophecy. Our noticing their presence in our midst makes clear to us that we are not totally destitute of gift and Spirit. Admittedly, an eighteen hundred-year history and the completed written Word stand at our side, and we can draw ever new refreshment and strength from both. These two advantages of our age should and can uphold our hearts in the place of the gift of prophecy, if we no longer find it among us as it was present in the first age. But precisely with respect to the two great advantages we have named it remains true that there is even now much insight into the apostolic and prophetic Word that does not derive from *personal* interpretation but from the Spirit of prophecy. Moreover, an interpretation of Scripture and a look at history from Scripture sometimes take us very close to the border of prophecy in the strict sense. We might indeed defend the claim that all true and proper prophecy necessary and profitable for the Church that might still come and that does not relate (as is the case in the prophecies [41] of Ac 11:27ff; 21:10-11) to purely earthly matters can be nothing other than exposition and application of the prophetic word deposited in the Holy Scriptures of the Old and New Testaments, the blossom, enjoyment, and fruit of the ancient and yet ever young Tree of Life, and of the future. All we need do is *esteem* the gifts and we find more than we thought or suspected. Yes, we acknowledge that the Lord's gracious presence and His Spirit of the future and of prophecy surround us like still waters, which we only notice when He opens our eyes and senses to attentiveness and thereby arouses the desire to drink from the flood that we behold and in which we were walking without receiving refreshment for our souls and purification from it.

VI. The Evangelists

§17. Eph 4:11 mentions the evangelists in third place among the offices bestowed by the ascended Christ on the Church [*Gemeinde*]. The double meaning of the word "prophecy" causes us to find much embarrassment and obscurity among those scholars whose wisdom we would consult concerning the New Testament prophets. Much more is this the case with respect to the evangelists, concerning whom we can by and large gain no satisfactory information. Moreover, the footholds in the New Testament text are too few for us easily to achieve clarity on this point. Apart from the already adduced text Eph 4:11 we find only two further passages in which the word "evangelist" appears. We wish to take a close look at the Ephesians text [42] and see what an examination of it might produce by way of shedding light on the office of evangelist in general. Yet Eph 4:11 by itself supplies nothing beyond the name "evangelist" unless we fasten on the *third* passage occupied by the office, which persuades us that it ranks immediately after the apostolic and prophetic offices in terms of dignity and importance.

Ac 8:12 ff in connection with 21:8

Deacons or almoners were elected in Jerusalem. When the congregation in Jerusalem was scattered, the deacons no longer had any serving of tables to do in Jerusalem, and so they too were scattered. A deacon in this category was the Philip who preached the Gospel in Samaria (Ac 8:4ff), to the finance minister from Ethiopia (Ac 8:35ff), and to all the cities of Judah (Ac 8:40), and who baptized the believers in Samaria and the finance minister from Ethiopia. (ἐπίστευσαν τῷ Φιλίππῳ εὐαγγελιζομένῳ τὰ περὶ τῆς βασιλείας, Ac 8:12a. διερχόμενος εὐηγγελίζετο τὰς πόλεις πάσας, Ac 8:40). Scripture expressly testifies concerning him that he was one of the seven appointed to care for the poor in Jerusalem and that he was an evangelist. "We entered the house of Philip the evangelist, who was one of the seven [RSV]" (Εἰσελθόντες εἰς τὸν οἶκον Φιλίππου τοῦ εὐαγγελιστοῦ, ὄντος ἐκ τῶν ἑπτά, ἐμείναμεν παρ' αὐτῷ, Ac 21:8).

2 Tim 4:5

This is the second passage to consider after Eph 4:11. Luther's translation "Do the work of an evangelical preacher" does admittedly [43] somewhat veil the meaning of this text, but the Greek original clearly demonstrates that it has the same sense here as in the Ephesians passage. "Do the work of an evangelist, carry out your office honestly" ("Ἔργον ποίησον εὐαγγελιστοῦ, τὴν διακονίαν σου πληροφόρησον.). Timothy was, then, an evangelist, and perhaps we might find much enlightenment concerning the essence of the office of evangelist from a consideration of what Scripture relates concerning the life and work of Timothy.

Ac 16:1ff tells how Paul found Timothy in Lystra, circumcised him, and took him with him. From then on we find Timothy in company with Paul or closely connected to and vigorously working with him. In Ac 17:15 Timothy receives a command (ἐντολὴν) from Paul (although the word is directed in first place to those who had to transmit the command) and is thus Paul's servant. In Ac 19:22 he is also called "a servant [RSV helper] of Paul," διακονῶν (τῷ Παύλῳ). The verb "serve," διακονεῖν, occurs here in a sense broadly similar to the way the nouns "servant and deacon" are used in Lutheran congregations of those clergymen who are subordinate to their brothers in office and appointed as their servants and helpers (1 The 3:2 συνεργός ἡμῶν). In 1 Cor 4:17 Timothy appears as a servant of God in Corinth whom the Corinthians should obey on account of his connection with Paul. In 1 Cor 16:10 he receives the great praise, "he is doing the work of the Lord as I am [RSV]" (τὸ γὰρ ἔργον κυρίου ἐργάζεται ὡς κἀγώ). Phil 2:19ff expresses yet greater praise towards him. St Paul says he has no one who is so much of [44] one heart and mind (ἰσόψυχος) as himself, and that he is assisting him in the Gospel as a son with his father (ὡς πατρὶ τέκνον σὺν ἐμοὶ ἐδούλευσεν εἰς τὸ εὐαγγέλιον). In 1 Tim 4:13f and 2 Tim 1:6 he is encouraged to stir up the gift that was in him through the laying on of hands of Paul and the presbytery. In 1 Tim 5:19ff Timothy appears as vocator, ordinator, and judge of presbyters, and in 1 Tim 6:13-14 he is commanded to remain faithful to the ministry entrusted to him until Christ's reappearance.

A comparison of the two evangelists Philip and Timothy will leave us in no doubt that the content of their sermons was essentially the same. It is also apparent that both stood under the oversight and control of apostles. Yet we shall also find some differences all of which are explicable in terms of the varying circumstances of time and needs of the congregations in whose midst they worked.

Philip was elected and ordained as a deacon in Jerusalem, but nothing is reported of how he became an evangelist. As we read the introduction to his career given in Ac 8:4, he seems entirely at home among the other scattered believers who "went about preaching the word" (διῆλθον εὐαγγελιζόμενοι τὸν λόγον). Not even the miracles mentioned in vv 6 and 7 would justify regarding him as special since other Christians at that time also possessed extraordinary gifts of the Holy Spirit. Only vv 26, 39, and 40 manifest factors that would prompt [45] us to ascribe Philip's service as an evangelist not to a merely human decision freely taken by himself in love but to some immediate, divine impulse from the Lord. On this basis we could consider him inspired for his office in a similar way as were the apostles in their greater measure and for wider circles. Should we wish to hold to the notion that both Philip and the other evangelists mentioned in Ac 8:4 (if we may label them thus) might have had a commission from the apostles for all that they did, it would still remain odd that not a single syllable of Scripture refers to this commission. This factor most strongly prompts the belief that, although Philip was indeed an evangelist, he should nevertheless not quite be ranked with the later evangelists, for example, with Timothy. There is no indication that he had an orderly connection with the apostles in general or with one of them in particular. While harmony with them is in evidence, it is freer in kind, less marked humanly speaking by signs of organization, and what catches the attention is his immediate contact with the miraculously intervening Lord. The Lord makes Philip an evangelist, but even though the latter acts under the impulse of the Spirit, he joyfully bows to apostolic control when it appears on the stage.

Things look quite different in the case of Timothy. He is—with recourse to a testimony of the brethren (ἐμαρτυρεῖτο ὑπὸ τῶν ἐν Λύστροις καὶ Ἰκονίῳ ἀδελφῶν, Ac 16:2)—elected by Paul, ordained by him and the entire presbytery, receives a special grace of office, is in utmost contact with and in obedience to an apostle, and we see him [46] serving St Paul as a son does a father (ὡς πατρὶ τέκνον δουλεῦον). Notwithstanding eminent great gifts, with respect to which he likely did not take second place to Philip (he may indeed also have the gift of miracles), he is no longer, as was Philip, illumined around by the first dawn of the kingdom of God. In his case we find the service of evangelist less under the immediate impulse of the Holy Spirit, but rather humanly speaking more developed, more limited, and more organized. We have here already an evangelist of the full apostolic day; the dominant factor in his ministry is not his being divinely overwhelmed, but a transfiguration and taking up of the human factor in the divine tasks of spreading the kingdom. We might see in Philip the nascent office of evangelist, in Timothy the fully formed office.

As the evangelist he is meant to be, Timothy is depicted and portrayed like no other servant of the Word outside the circle of evangelists. He furnishes the standard by which we can measure other servants of the Gospel in the New Testament. We find many who have similar tasks to Timothy and who may therefore like him claim the name of evangelist. Let us remember above all Titus, a Greek by birth, purposely not circumcised (as was Timothy), who entered into almost as close a relationship with Paul as that enjoyed by Timothy. In 2 Cor 2:13 Paul calls Titus his "brother" in a sense and context that permits us to conclude high esteem on the apostle's part. In the seventh chapter the same impartial mouth pronounces great praise in his regard, a praise similar to that lavished on Timothy in Phil 2:19ff. Cf. also 2 Cor 8:23. If we still entertain doubts [47] on this score, Titus's situation clearly set forth in the letter to him makes us certain that for his circles on Crete he exercised the office of evangelist no less than did Timothy in other areas.

Alongside Titus we find *John Mark* (Ac 12:35; 13:5, ὑπηρέτης. εἶχον δὲ καὶ Ἰωάννην ὑπηρέτην 15:36ff; 13:13; Col 4:10; Philem 24; 2 Tim 4:11) as evangelist of Paul and Peter. Mark's offence, which is related in Ac 15:36ff, did not permanently dissolve his relationship with Paul. St Paul seems to have been in the right over against St Barnabas, and for that reason at his departure the congregation [*Gemeine*] commended him to the Lord along with Silas, and Mark returned contritely to his leader.

As servants of Paul (διακονοῦντες τῷ Παυλῳ) we find *Silas* in Ac 17:15 and *Erastus* alongside Timothy in Ac 19:22. Several companions and assistants of Paul are mentioned in Ac 20:4. The following are described in situations that enable and indeed oblige us to ascribe to them the office and service of evangelist in the image if not in the measure of Timothy: in Rom 16:3, 9 Aquila (admittedly in company with Prisca, which is not hard to explain) and Urbanus; and in Eph 6:21 and Col 4:7 Tychichus (πιστὸς διάκονος καὶ σύνδουλος ἐν κυρίῳ). Quenstedt (*op.cit.*, p. 80) refers also to the headings of St Paul's letters, in which he often greets the congregation together with the evangelist then standing at his side. 1 Cor 1:1 (*Sosthenes*, Ac 18:17?); 2 Cor 1:1; Col 1:1; Phil 1:1; 1 The 1:1 (Silvanus-Silas); Philem 1.

[48] §18. Surprise has sometimes been expressed that the office of evangelist was lost almost without trace from the history of the

Church. There was a desire not to surrender to this disappearance of a holy office. The loss was blamed on the vision of those who examined the evidence, which was accordingly sharpened. And yet scholars did not see the obvious, which proceeds as a corollary from all the passages hitherto listed. The evangelists were an office of the first age, present entirely for the first foundation and spread of the kingdom of God, originating with the apostles, working under their supervision, according to their direction, and at their side, dying and dying out with them or at any rate shortly after them, just as its light disappears soon after the sun. An evangelist is an apostolic assistant, a forerunner and companion of an apostle, one who labors in his wake. The evangelists of the New Testament appear thus and not otherwise, which explains why there were no more later on. In terms of its duration the office of evangelist in the strict sense was restricted to the apostolic age. When Eusebius speaks in his *History of the Church* (4^{13}.37; 5.10) of evangelists who were permeated by a divine zeal to imitate the apostles and who did their part for the spread of the kingdom of God, he does not dispute this. Apart from the fact that he speaks of them in 5.10 as a leftover ("At that time there were still some evangelists"), as but the last rays of suns that had already set, he emphatically does not say that the men whom he so justly praised belong in the same rank as the apostles' pupils of the New Testament. They were evangelists of second rank, just as [49] today we might do zealous missionaries the honor of placing them at the end of the series of evangelists, whose beginning is found in the apostolic age, whose offshoots are still there in the second century to become ever more weakly attested from then onwards.

> Note. Earlier writers have taken our view of the office of evangelist. Quenstedt says, *op.cit.*, §8, "The evangelists seem to have been companions, σύνεργοι καὶ συλλειτουργοί, or assistants of the apostles, inferior to them in rank and dignity, taken by them into some part of the sacred office, so that they either undertook the first planting of Christian doctrine or were charged with the work of irrigating and perfecting what the apostles had felicitously begun. Since the apostles lacked the capacity to do everything,

they availed themselves of the evangelists' deputizing or assisting labors in propagating the evangelical doctrine concerning Christ. Thus they were either the companions or legates or ambassadors of the apostles, whom they sent here or there or took along with them for the planting or pruning of the churches." Quenstedt could have omitted the "seem" [*videntur*], since either Timothy was not an evangelist, which is expressly stated, or an evangelist is what Timothy was and Quenstedt said.

§19. Mark was an evangelist in the sense set forth here, and his written Gospel surely had its source in his office as evangelist. As Peter's oral evangelist, he was enabled and authorized to write down the Gospel on which Peter had built congregations (cf Thiersch's *Versuch etc.*, p. 79). Quenstedt is also quite right to describe *Luke* as an evangelist on p. 79 (Col 4:14; 2 Tim 4:11; Philem 24), [50] for which reason his written Gospel might well have sprung from his office as did that of the evangelist Mark. The two men would accordingly first have been oral evangelists before becoming evangelists of the pen, even if we may not go quite so far as do Quenstedt and St Irenaeus by understanding the "brother" (οὗ ὁ ἔπαινος ἐν τῷ εὐαγγελίῳ διὰ πασῶν τῶν ἐκκλησιῶν) of 2 Cor 8:18 as a reference to St Luke.

> Note 1. We could if need be join Hugo Grotius in labeling the evangelists "traveling presbyters attached to no specific church" [*Presbyteri* περιοδευτὰι, *nulli certae ecclesiae affixi*], even though they do not bear this name in Holy Scripture.

> Note 2. The ἀδελφοὶ, ἀπόστολοι ἐκκλησιῶν named in 2 Cor 8:23 are not apostles *to* the congregations, but apostles or delegates *from* them.

VII. Presbyters and Bishops

§20. We find elders (presbyters) already in the Old Testament and among the Jews contemporary with Christ. As a self-evident feature of communal life, they smoothly blend over from the theocratic congregation of the Old Testament to the churchly congregations of the New Covenant. In the process, though, we are unable to state where and when the Lord and His apostles pronounced that this feature of Old Testament organization should be carried on in the New Testament kingdom of grace. Entirely without preparation the office and name of elders meets us [51] for the first time in Ac 11:30. Wherever a flock of God gathers, elders arise according to unavoidable need. In Ac 14:23 we find the apostles self-evidently installing them into the congregations ("They"–Paul and Barnabas–"appointed elders for them in every church" [RSV]). And we find the office of elder treated in the apostolic letters as a universal institution thoroughly suited to the Christian congregations (1 Tim, Tit, 1 Pet etc.). We cannot produce a precise apostolic text in which the office of elders is commanded for all times. Yet it belonged without doubt to the universal apostolic practice and many apostolic commands and directives presuppose it and treat it as foundational. The whole subsequent time of the Church honored this practice to such an extent that it universally retained it. There was a universal certain conviction that no better arrangement could be found, and the experience of the centuries confirmed this assurance. The Lutheran Church, too, preserved the office of elder in such a way that, while the name of the office changed here and there, its essence and the commands affecting it did not.

§21. The apostles attribute the name "presbyter" (elder) not only to the elders they set in place but also to themselves. St Paul speaks in 1 Tim 4:14 of Timothy's having received his gift through the laying on of hands of the *presbytery* or college of elders (μετὰ ἐπιθέσεως τῶν χειρῶν τοῦ πρεσβυτερίου) and says in 2 Tim 1:6 that the gift was in Timothy through the laying on of *his* hands (διὰ τῆς ἐπιθέσεως τῶν χειρῶν μου). [52], Yet, given the fact that the name "presbyter" also encompasses the apostles, these two apparently contradictory passages in fact agree because we count St Paul himself within the presbyteral college at whose head he carried out Timothy's ordination. We deduce the apostles' reckoning themselves as elders not merely from their position vis-à-vis the first congregation of Jerusalem which was actually (or at least implicitly) that of other elders towards congregations, but also from St Peter's naming himself the *fellow elder* in 1 Pet 5:1 (πρεσβυτέρους τοὺς ἐν ὑμῖν παρακαλῶ ὁ συμπρεσβύτερος) and St John's naming himself simply "the elder" (2 Jn 1: ὁ πρεσβύτερος ἐκλεκτῇ κυρίᾳ, 3 Jn 1 ὁ πρεσβύτερος Γαΐῳ). Since St Peter names himself a fellow elder of all the elders who worked among the elect pilgrims in Pontus, Galatia, Cappadocia, Asia, and Bithynia, we might conclude that the apostles accordingly ascribed to themselves membership in all presbyteral colleges of the far-flung congregations. Yet this conception would not overturn the claim that the apostles had the office of elder. By virtue of their universal call that extended over all congregations and of their accompanying power and gift, they would have had seat and voice in all colleges of elders, but their seat and their voice would have been those of an elder. The presbyterate would then embrace both them and the lowliest congregational elder in a single office and a single dignity. This solidarity explains [53] why in Ac 15:2ff. they do not shrink from forming, together with the elders, the core authoritative group within the first synod, nor from becoming, together with them, the governing authority for the congregations in Jerusalem and at other places. But if the apostles and the ordinary elders constituted to a certain degree *one* college and *one* presbyterate and bore a single office, then no one can contest our claim that those are to be reckoned to the presbyterate who stand in between the apostles and the elders, namely the fellow workers and servants of the apostles (συνεργοι και διάκονοι τῶν ἀποστόλων), the *evangelists*. In considering this remark one may well assert that there is in the New Testament only *one* office for the *governance* and *feeding* of the congregation, the presbyterate. For the diaconate is an entirely different office, which exists hardly anywhere in present-day Christendom in its original form and competence, and which widely differs from those presbyters who were labeled "deacons" in the Lutheran Church. This would nicely justify the parallel claim of the Lutheran Church that the office of the New Testament is essentially one. Apostles, evangelists, and presbyters (as an extraordinary office, the prophets do not belong in this sequence) have a single goal, a single path, a single chief means of operating. Yet, without detriment to what each holder of the single office has in common, there are "levels" [*Stufen*] within the single office ordered in such a way that those above always have a certain precedence over those beneath. One might almost make a comparison akin to that between patriarchs, [54] bishops, and presbyters of a later age, if one did not thereby sail too close to the doctrine of the Romanists who extend the priestly office from Pope to priest but so emphasize the distance between the two that they thrust what they have in common into the shadows and the background.

§22. There is a second name for the presbyterate in the New Testament. The presbyters are also named *bishops*.

In Ac 20:28 St Paul says to the *elders* of Ephesus, whom he had summoned to Miletus, "Take heed to yourselves and to the whole flock among which the Holy Spirit has placed you as *bishops* to feed the church [*Gemeine*] of God, which he purchased through his own blood." Thus the Holy Spirit placed the elders as bishops. One set of persons has two sets of names, yet only a single office.

In Phil 1:1 the *bishops* and *servants* of the congregation of Philippi are addressed. Thus the congregation of Philippi did not have merely one bishop, a number of elders, and a number of servants, of which Paul would be emphasizing the first and the third while passing silently over the second group. Rather, it had several bishops, i.e., elders, and a number of servants or deacons. No one can take the text otherwise, and hence everyone will have to concede that the names bishop and presbyter are used interchangeably.

We find entirely the same use of language in 1 Tim 3:1ff. Vss. 1-7 list the qualifications for the episcopate (ἐπισκοπὴ), while vss. 8ff. state those for the diaconate. Why are those for the presbyterate [55] not named[14]? Because presbyterate and episcopate are one and the same thing. Hence in 1 Tim 4:14 all the bishops of Lystra are subsumed under the name presbytery, and in 1 Tim 5:17 the name presbyter suddenly appears and from that point on is retained in vss. 19, 20, & 21.

Any remaining doubt [concerning our conclusions] will completely disappear on closer examination of the passage Tit 1:5-7. In v. 5 the apostle says that he left Titus in Crete in order to complete what Paul had not achieved by supplying the cities with *elders*, as he had commanded him. But a presbyter must be without reproach etc.; for a *bishop* must be without reproach as a steward of God (Τούτου χάριν ἀπέλιπόν σε ἐν Κρήτῃ, ἵνα τὰ λείποντα ἐπιδιορθώσῃ καὶ καταστήσῃς κατὰ πόλιν πρεσβυτέρους, ὡς ἐγώ σοι διεταξάμην, εἴ τίς ἐστιν ἀνέγκλητος, μιᾶς γυναικὸς ἀνήρ, τέκνα ἔχων πιστά, μὴ ἐν κατηγορίᾳ ἀσωτίας ἢ ἀνυπότακτα. δεῖ γὰρ τὸν ἐπίσκοπον ἀνέγκλητον εἶναι ὡς θεοῦ οἰκονόμον, etc. etc.). If this passage does not prove the matter, then I don't know what in all the world might have power of proof. So let no one set himself the task of proving that in the New Testament episcopate and presbyterate are anything other than two sets of names, of which the one alludes to the calling and the other to the dignity of the same office and the same persons, the one deriving from the activity of the office, the other from the personal maturity of the one who holds it.

§23. The question *who appointed* the presbyters in the congregations and what share fell to the congregations in electing and placing the presbyters is answered [56] by the biblical passages Ac 14:24, 20:17ff., 1 Tim 3:1-15, and Tit. 1:55ff., which must be the sole texts relevant to the point at issue.

In Ac 14:23 we find that Paul and Barnabas appointed elders for the new congregations in Lystra, Iconium, and Antioch (in Pisidia) without any mention being made of the slightest participation by the congregations in the election of the elders. And not only did the apostles themselves appoint shepherds for the congregations without any active participation being ascribed to the latter in the election and appointment, but precisely in the second most plainly pertinent passage Tit 1:5ff. we meet the same state of affairs with respect to an *evangelist*. St Paul left his pupil Titus behind on Crete in order that he might continue and conclude the work that the apostle had begun. And in what did this work consist? In *appointing* presbyters city by city in keeping with the definite norm prescribed for him by the apostle (ἵνα καταστήσῃς κατὰ πόλιν πρεσβυτέρους, ὡς ἐγώ σοι διεταξάμην·). The passage 1 Tim 3:1ff. is to be understood along precisely these lines. As pupils of the apostles, evangelists could, like apostles, appoint elders and continue and complete the work begun by the apostles. Whoever was appointed by them–or by apostles–as presbyter of a congregation was able and obliged according to Ac 20:28 to regard himself as appointed by the Holy Spirit. His office was indeed not like that of the apostles, who could say, as did St Paul in Gal 1:1, that they were appointed neither from man nor through man, but he could nevertheless say with utmost truth that he was a presbyter of the congregation *through* man but not *from* man. Just make a mental leap [57] into Titus' work on Crete or Timothy's in and around Ephesus in order to register the role of the congregations in the appointment of presbyters. Titus, for example, was to appoint presbyters city by city for the Christians present [on the island, officers] who, be it noted, were to be taken from the number of the congregational members themselves. Did he, did Timothy within his circle, or did the apostles on the universal level, have such detailed knowledge of all congregational members that they could test those Christians who applied for the bishop's office (for according to 1 Tim 3:1 men could apply) according to the touchstone of the norms given in Tit 1 and 1 Tim 3, or, if no one did apply, so that they could detect suitable men among the silent crowd? If they themselves lacked the necessary insight, how could they get to know the candidates for the holy office except from the testimony of the Christians from whose midst they arose and in whose midst they should exercise the office? After all, according to Ac 16:2, Timothy himself was selected by Paul with the testimony of the brethren in Lystra and Iconium (ἐμαρτυρεῖ το ὑπὸ τῶν ἐν Λύστροις καὶ Ἰκονίῳ ἀδελφῶν). Whoever thinks this over will find that we have here the widest elbowroom for congregational participation in the appointment of presbyters. The congregation's testimony could be given in weaker or stronger terms, with or without the express wish for information concerning a particular man. Petitions, acclamations for this one or that one, a respectful suggestion, a veto or refusal [of nomination]– all of these possibilities can be imagined within the parameters of congregational testimony. It would be surprising if [58] the congregations did not already participate in elections earlier than– as Bellarmine says–at the time of the council of Nicea, and we cannot be in the least surprised when, at the time of Cyprian in North Africa, the greatest measure of influence in elections must be ascribed to the congregations. The congregations' elbowroom is large or small according to circumstances; but the actual appointing, the final decisive voice must in the end of the day belong to Timothy, Titus, Paul, for it is written of *them* that they did the appointing. The congregation could obviously make a mistake, elect in a fit of passion, be misled, be disposed in favor of heretics. Should Titus, Timothy etc. yield to a congregation in such cases? By no means! Titus did the appointing, authority was given to him not for the ruin but for the well-being of the congregations; he was obliged to use this authority for their well-being. There is admittedly a difference between the apostles' *"ordaining"* (χειροτονεῖν, Ac 14:23) and the "appointing" (ἵνα καταστήσῃς) authorized in Tit 1:5. The former must indicate both the greater trust and the higher authority of the apostles, and yet neither of the two words places any power in the hands of the congregation, but the final appraisal and decision concerning the man to be ordained rested with the one who had the decision to "appoint." At any rate the work was his and it was left to his love, wisdom, and responsibility to determine the measure in which the congregations might play a role in the process.

Since each of those congregations was given its presbyters from its own midst, they were in a completely different situation from our own congregations. Not only were [59] they far more in the stream of original Christian life, more familiar with the destination to which they were being led and the means being used to get them there, but they also had a genuine knowledge of the candidates, and there was no need of any risky trial sermons or letters of recommendation from afar etc. Conversely, what kind of congregations do we have and what do they consist of! How should they be in a position to judge the competence and worthiness of candidates who do not even come from their midst! To say nothing of the spirit of our age that could lead in the election of a presbyter to the same agitations as occur in the election of a state assemblyman! No! An absolute right of election on the part of the congregation is not only unapostolic but also highly dangerous, a way to drive Christ out of the congregations through a majority of votes and to open wide the gate to the Baal of this world. Just as presbyters (apostles, evangelists etc.) appointed presbyters, with involvement of the congregations being left to their wise discretion, so let it happen today. Be it left to the appointing presbyter (bishop), let it be recommended and even commanded him, to heed the just wishes of the congregations. Let it be permitted and not forbidden the congregations to bring to bear their "testimony" concerning the one to be elected and to express their wishes, but let them also acknowledge that it is not *their* right to strive against the judgment of the one who does the appointing (i.e., the bishop). The one who does the appointing can make a mistake, and his conduct can be brought to the synod; a whole congregation must not be helplessly handed over to the sovereign dealings of a single man. But if the one who does the appointing is honest and up to his job, he has an interest [60] in discharging his office well, and his governance must work more blessing for the congregations than that of an easily misled mob who have no idea what they are to have and receive from the office. If the first congregations did not elect, if the decision was there in the hand of a single wise and pious presbyter, how much more must the same hold good for our desolate congregations.

§24. We find many allusions in Holy Scripture to the *tasks* that the presbyters had to perform. We wish to leave out of consideration at this juncture their relationship to poor relief and those who care for the poor, which we can learn from Ac 11:30. We shall have further opportunity in the course of these aphorisms to express ourselves in greater detail on this point. We also wish to defer to another place discussion of the activity of presbyters at synods according to Ac 15:2. For now we fix our gaze only on the proper sphere of the presbyterate, discovering the following points:

> In 1 Tim 5:17 and 1 Thess 5:12 we find its relationship with the congregation characterized by the expression *preside* (προιστάναι). They are to *preside*, which–as emerges from 1 Pet 5:2-3—does not mean *rule*.

> In Ac 20:28 and 1 Pet 5:2 the task of the presbyters is characterized in general as a pasturing (ποιμαίνειν), so that it can be broken down into feeding, protecting, leading, and healing. For the entire activity of a shepherd engaged in pasturing [sheep] splits up into these individual tasks.

> [61] The expression "steward" (οἰκονόμος), which we find applied to all levels of the presbyterate in 1 Cor 4:1 ("This is how one should regard us–namely, Paul, Cephas, Apollos–, as servants of Christ and stewards of the mysteries of God" [RSV]) and with particular reference to bishops or presbyters in Tit 1:7, points to

the caring, feeding, and drink-supplying activity of the holy office of a shepherd. As a steward is placed over his master's servants and a manager allots to each of his master's workers their food and daily wage, so are presbyters placed over the holy mysteries and treasures of God that are hid from the world, and their office is *rightly to divide* God's word and sacrament–for what else should God's treasures and mysteries be, so far as they are to be administered by presbyters? Therefore Paul writes to Timothy in 2 Tim 2:15, "Study to shew thyself approved unto God, a workman that needeth not to be ashamed, rightly dividing the word of truth" [KJV] (σπούδασον σεαυτὸν δόκιμον παραστῆσαι τῷ θεῷ, ἐργάτην ἀνεπαίσχυντον, ὀρθοτομοῦντα τὸν λόγον τῆς ἀληθείας.). It does indeed appear as though this obligation of presbyters rightly to divide the word of God had not been imposed on all who shared this office, since in 1 Tim 5:17f. those who labored in the word and in doctrine were distinguished from the others and accorded preference over them ("Let the elders who rule well be considered worthy of double honor, especially those who labor *in preaching and teaching*" [RSV], μάλιστα οἱ κοπιῶντες ἐν λόγῳ καὶ διδασκαλίᾳ) and also because elsewhere emphasis is placed on the *teachers* as an especially gifted class of congregational members who were not necessarily entrusted with the office of elder. On the basis of this perception, in their remarkable church constitution the Bohemian Brethren separated teachers and elders from one another, and in the same sense the Romans appoint special preachers at larger churches. We absolutely do not wish to deny that, as many presbyters labored and expended themselves less in doctrine (οἱ κοπιῶντες ἐν λόγῳ καὶ διδασκαλίᾳ!), they achieved more in liturgical and sacramental service, in pastoral care and in directing congregational matters etc. Yet this concession does not impel us to assert against explicit passages of Holy Scripture and against the sense of what has already been alleged that in the areas of the holy office where they specialized they would have had no opportunity to divide the word, whether wrongly or rightly.

Even among ourselves the gift of teaching and preaching has not become so common that one should not wish for many elders to be relieved of their duty to teach and to preach in order thereby to apply themselves with all the greater energy to the parts of the office for which they are gifted. Without standing in the pulpit they would still have ample scope for demonstrating their gift of teaching in pastoral care etc. Yet 1 Tim 3:2 expressly commands that they *must* have the gift of teaching. Already at the time when the office of elder parted company from that of the deacons, Ac 6:4, the former is placed in the service of the word and prayer (viz., liturgical service). "But we will devote ourselves to prayer and the ministry of the [63] word" [RSV], ἡμεῖς δὲ τῇ προσευχῇ καὶ τῇ διακονίᾳ τοῦ λόγου προσκαρτερήσομεν. But if anyone would apply the sense of this passage not only to the apostolate, there are nevertheless still other passages that cannot be dismissed and in which the office of the word is ascribed to the elders. In Eph 4:11, where the offices of the Holy Spirit bequeathed by Christ are listed, we find shepherds and teachers connected by a single definite article (τοὺς δὲ ποιμένας καὶ διδασκάλους), so that we acknowledge in both words a double reference to the same persons, and we must recognize that the office of pastor and that of teacher belong together. In 1 The 5:12[15] it seems obligatory to interpret the expression "who labor among you" (κοπιῶντες ἐν ὑμῖν) entirely on the basis of the same, only more definite expression in 1 Tim 5:17, "those who labor in the word and in doctrine" (οἱ κοπιῶντες ἐν λόγῳ καὶ διδασκαλίᾳ), and to refer it at least in large part to the work that the elders discharged in the actual teaching office. Most convincing of all, though, is the passage of St Paul in 1 Tim 3:2, which we have already adduced. It is here expressly demanded that aspirants to the presbyterate must be *able to teach* (Δεῖ οὖν τὸν ἐπίσκοπον διδακτικὸν εἶναι). And the passage 2 Tim 2:2 reads like an explanation of this verse: "And what you have heard from me before many witnesses entrust to faithful men who *will be able to teach others also*" [RSV] (Ἃ ἤκουσας παρ' ἐμοῦ διὰ πολλῶν μαρτύρων, ταῦ τα παράθου πιστοῖς ἀνθρώποις, οἵτινες ἱκανοὶ ἔσονται καὶ ἑτέρους διδάξαι). On this basis we may indeed concede: (1) that there could be people who had and exercised the gift of teaching even outside the presbyterate [64]; (2) that the strength of many presbyters did not lie precisely in the work of the word and public doctrine, nor were they especially active in this area. And yet we must also maintain (3) that according to the apostle's meaning a presbyter had in a certain sense to be able to teach. The separation wrought by the Bohemian Brethren might thus be far too sharp and at all events it turned out to the disadvantage of their presbyterate.

We also find New Testament passages pertaining to the protecting and governing aspects of the presbyterate. 1 The 5:12 says of those who presided, i.e., of the elders of the congregation at Thessalonica, that they *set right the minds* of the Christians given over to their care, or, as Luther translates, "admonished them" (νουθετοῦντας). Therein lies at all events an element of governance, of protection against internal dangers. Tit 1:9 demands of the future presbyter that he "hold firm to the sure word as taught, so that he may be able to give instruction in sound doctrine and also to confute those who contradict it" [RSV] (Ἀντεχόμενον τοῦ κατὰ τὴν διδαχὴν πιστοῦ λόγου, ἵνα δυνατὸς ᾖ καὶ παρακαλεῖν ἐν τῇ διδασκαλίᾳ τῇ ὑγιαινούσῃ καὶ τοὺς ἀντιλέγοντας ἐλέγχειν). "For there are many insubordinate men, empty talkers and deceivers, especially the circumcision party; they must be silenced (οὓς δεῖ ἐπιστομίζειν), since they are upsetting whole families by teaching for base gain what they have no right to teach" (Tit 1:10-11 [RSV]). This verse also unmistakably expresses how an elder ought, as much as in him lies, to protect his congregation from the dangers of spiritual seduction and to lead them towards eternal life [65] through many dangers and threats of seduction. Both aspects, along with the entire duty of a shepherd, are contained in the simple epithet of 1 Pet 5:2, "exercising oversight," ἐπισκοποῦντες. "Feed the flock of God which is among you, taking the oversight thereof, not by constraint, but willingly"–(ποιμάνατε τὸ ἐν ὑμῖν ποίμνιον τοῦ Θεοῦ, ἐπισκοποῦντες μὴ ἀναγκαστῶς, ἀλλ' ἑκουσίως). For what kind of oversight over a flock would it be if the sheep's own slip-ups and the dangers threatening from the wolf were not foreseen, not noticed, not resisted, not avoided?

In the just-mentioned epithet "exercising oversight" (ἐπισκοποῦντες) we also find included the healing and helping element in the office of elder, but believe that under this heading belongs especially the office of prayer, which took place not only publicly but also at sick beds, formal directives for the latter being given at Jas 5:14. The official prayer of the elders and the hope of their being heard, even apart from the use of oil, have deep roots in this glorious passage. "Is any among you sick? Let him call for the elders of the church, and let them pray over him, anointing him with oil in the name of the Lord; and the prayer of faith will save the sick man, ...and if he has committed sins, he will be forgiven" [RSV]–(ἀσθενεῖ τις ἐν ὑμῖν; προσκαλεσάσθω τοὺς πρεσβυτέρους τῆς ἐκκλησίας, καὶ προσευξάσθωσαν ἐπ' αὐτὸν etc.).

§25. The preceding makes sufficiently plain how dear and worthy is the word of the apostle, "If anyone aspires to the office of bishop [*Bischofsamt*], he desires a [66] noble task" (1 Tim 3:1 RSV] (καλοῦ ἔργου ἐπιθυμεῖ). The *qualifications* are in keeping with the office itself. The Lord summarizes them briefly in the Gospel and names them "mouth and wisdom" (στόμα καὶ σοφίαν, Lk 21:15), and what He briskly pinpoints we find named and interpreted more largely in 1 Tim 3:1ff., Tit 1:7ff., 1 Pet 5:1ff. We do not wish to deal with these qualifications here but at most to refer to what the present writer has said on this topic in his contributions on pastoral theology in the Erlangen *Zeitschrift für Protestantismus und Kirche* of 1847/48. Everything that ought to be said does not belong in the first instance here in these aphorisms, which are directed more towards the outside as they deal with the structure of the Church and her offices.

§26. We may stay more on topic when we draw attention

to Holy Scripture's surely according certain *privileges* to the presbyters.

> According to 1 The 5:12 they should be *recognized* in their office, their exertion and work (Ἐρωτῶμεν δὲ ὑμᾶς, ἀδελφοί, εἰδέναι τοὺς κοπιῶντας ἐν ὑμῖν); for the sake of their work they should stand the higher in the *love of the congregation,* v. 13 (ἡγεῖσθαι αὐτοὺς ὑπερ ἐκπερισσοῦ ἐν ἀγάπῃ διὰ τὸ ἔργον αὐτῶν). According to 1 Tim 5:17 presbyters who preside well, especially if they labor in the word and doctrine, should be held worthy of double honor, and this is to be expounded not simply in terms of honor in word and conduct, but also in terms of an ample livelihood. (Cf. 2 Cor 11:8; Gal 6:6ff.; 2 Tim 2:6). Vs. 19 even accords them a certain [67] privilege before an ecclesiastical *court*: "Never admit any charge against an elder except on the evidence of two or three witnesses" (κατὰ πρεσβυτέρου κατηγορίαν μὴ παραδέχου, ἐκτὸς εἰ μὴ ἐπὶ δύο ἢ☐ τριῶν μαρτύρων). This privilege is certainly thoroughly in order since an elder easily and to a greater degree than others arouses the hatred of the unclean and the impure and wickedness delights to mobilize itself with lies and spite against men of this office. It also fits the dignity of this office that folk proceed slowly in judging its holders. And yet it is also commanded that erring elders convicted by two or three witnesses be punished in the presence of all, so that the others may stand in fear; 1 Tim 5:20. (Τοὺς ἁμαρτάνοντας ἐνώπιον πάντων ἔλεγχε, ἵνα καὶ οἱ λοιποὶ φόβον ἔχωσιν).

§27. We may ask whether, already according to the testimony of Holy Scripture, one member stood out from the presbyteral college as a *primus inter pares* over the others, thus whether *traces of an episcopal office in the sense of the post-apostolic period are already to be found in Holy Scripture?* Since each congregation had not just one but several elders and these formed a totality, a college, it stands to reason that the very rules of order necessitated a *primus inter pares* [first among equals], a presiding officer [*Präses*], that differing gifts caused one to attract attention over another and likewise one over all and that the influence of one[16] in particular would be bound to be the greater [68] the holier the dispositions of all, the less pride, envy, and jealousy, the more love and wisdom ruled hearts. No one somewhat capable of picturing the circumstances will deny that for such reasons, and especially because so much was taking place within and amongst the congregations, an episcopal office in the post-apostolic sense was humanly and naturally in the process of formation already in the apostolic age itself. And this is also what we find. When after his release from prison St Peter seeks out the Christians gathered in the house of John Mark and charges them on his departure, "Tell this to James and to the brethren" (Ac 12:17 RSV, Ἀπαγγείλατε Ἰακώβῳ καὶ τοῖς ἀδελφοῖς ταῦτα); when at the first synod in Jerusalem James, marked by obvious signs of prestige, formulates and expresses the synod's decision in Ac 15:19 (διὸ ἐγὼ κρίνω etc.); when in Ac 21:8, immediately after his arrival in Jerusalem, Paul along with his companions "goes in" to James (εἰσῄει ὁ Παῦλος σὺν ἡμῖν πρὸς Ἰάκωβον) and all the elders gather at his place (πάντες τε παρεγένοντο οἱ πρεσβύτεροι); when (if we are not mistaken) in Gal. 1:19 & 2:9 *the same* James is mentioned in a way that assures him a certain precedence (or however one may wish to name it) in Jerusalem: all these single observations may well confirm the ancient, established report that James was the first bishop of Jerusalem.

As already stated above, in Phil 1:1 the *bishops* of Philippi are greeted and in 4:3 a man is addressed as Paul's "true yokefellow" [RSV] (σύζυγος γνήσιος), so that one [69] could come to the opinion that a reference is being made here to a prominent member of the presbyteral college.

The seven *stars* and *angels* of the churches [*Gemeinden*], to whom in Revelation the Lord directs His letters through the hand of John, merit special attention. See Rv 1;20; 2:1, 8, 12, 18; 3:1, 7, 14. We see in Ac 20:17 ff. that there were in Ephesus presbyters or bishops whom Paul summoned to himself at Miletus. In Rv 2:1 the Lord Himself addresses one of them as star and angel of the church [*Gemeinde*]. For the thoroughly ministerial status and high responsibility of the "angel," which is apparent from all the letters of Revelation, precludes our assuming, as some do, that by the "angel" we are to understand none of the bishops or presbyters, but some other member of the congregation. The text can only be speaking of a shepherd and indeed of one to whom the rest of the congregation in its entirety is in a certain measure and manner entrusted. We thus have here at all events at the end of the first century an instance of the Lord Himself if not commanding, at any rate recognizing a dignity and position not dissimilar to that of a bishop of the subsequent period.

If we recall in this context how we have already spoken above of "rungs" [*Stufen*] within the presbyterate, and if we acquire a firmer grasp of what has just been said, this evidence will speak for a certain exercise of oversight in the congregations. To say nothing of the apostles, we would simply point to the evangelists. Admittedly, we are not obliged to deduce any superiority of Timothy or Titus over other elders from their being commissioned to appoint elders in 1 Tim 3 and Tit 1. [70] After all, a presbyter can make presbyters, the ordainer raising the one ordained to an equality of rank with himself. Yet it also seems that we must assume that Timothy and Titus had something to say over already appointed presbyters, that in certain circles they had jurisdiction over them and their congregations. Simply read Paul's letters to Timothy and Titus with this issue in mind and see what kind of charges and instructions the apostle gives them. If we consider it in its scope over entire congregations, the very command to elect, test, and ordain elders (1 Tim 5:22) will appear as something momentous that can only have achieved the loftiest prestige for the two evangelists in the congregations. And then factor in those passages (1 Tim 5:19, 20, 21) where Timothy is set before the presbyters as a judge who has to hear witnesses, pronounce judgments, and punish guilty presbyters in the presence of all! How can one interpret this other than in terms over a dignity rising over the other presbyters? Even the serious and solemn manner in which Timothy is admonished (1 Tim 5:21) to exercise his office of oversight (cf 1 Pet 5:2) points to the great powers given him and to the great duties placed on him.

And yet the passages adduced thus far are of two kinds. Those taken from the Acts of the Apostles, from Phil 1, and from Revelation speak of the superintendency over single congregations and their presbyters that arose from the college of presbyters. Conversely, the passages from the Pastoral Epistles show us in [71] Timothy and Titus ordinators, visitors, and evangelists for large stretches of territory and many congregations. These are indeed two highly different things. When, for example, we find three, five, or eight presbyters placed in many of our present congregations, order demands that they come to an arrangement among themselves about the conduct of business, that each one is assigned his own range of tasks, and that one of them be put in charge. Here arises a *primus inter pares* [first among equals], the "angel" of a congregation concerning whom one might simply ask whether the office that has become his in an orderly way has the same recognition with the Lord as had the respective angel in each of the seven churches [*Gemeinden*]. It's different with Timothy and Titus. They traverse towns, give the emerging congregations elders and ordinances, visit the standing congregations, and exercise jurisdiction, and this in virtue of an apostolic command, so that anyone who is disobedient to them is disobedient to the apostles. Here we have a sphere of activity that encompasses not one but many congregations; here we have offices for the firmer establishment and at the same time for the extension of the Church.

Many misgivings strike us in this context. Everywhere in the New Testament we see that the holy office begets the congregations, never that the office—also in its particular version of office of elder—is simply a transferral of congregational rights and authority where the congregation gives the office. The office stands in the midst of the congregations as a fruitful tree that contains its own seed. The statement that it replenishes itself remains true even when taking into account, as we did above, congregational participation in the election and calling of [72] elders. So long as the presbyterate remains responsible for the examination and ordination (and also for the installation) of presbyters in all stages of the calling process (and how should it lose this responsibility?), the thesis is correct and defensible that the presbyterate replenishes and propagates itself from person to person and from generation to generation. Those who have it transmit it further, and whoever has it passed on to him by its occupants has it by divine right [*von Gottes wegen*]. Something simultaneously human and divine is happening here, as is generally the case in God's household of grace, and from this perspective we might understand and supplement Caspar Ziegler's opinion in his *liber commentarius de episcopis* (Nuremberg, 1686), p. 21. We here come to the element of truth in the idea of *succession* to which most Christian churches of the earth adhere. It is not enough that an elder be rightly elected and called, but those who were elders before him must acknowledge him as qualified and approve his election, and they must confer the office on him under prayer and the laying on of hands. Only then is he what he is meant to be. Precisely the examples of Timothy and Titus prove this both backwards and forwards. The office is a river of blessing that gushes forth from the apostles to their pupils and from these pupils further yet down to the ages.

It is certain that the apostles' pupils had the apostolic mandate to propagate their office. "You then, my son, be strong," writes Paul to Timothy in 2 Tim 2:1-2, "in the grace that is in Christ Jesus, and what you have heard from me before many witnesses entrust to faithful men who will be able to [73] teach others also" [RSV]. Any proof that the apostles' pupils in turn mandated others to travel around as they did, organize congregations, and appoint presbyters, would be tantamount to proving the apostolicity and divinity of the succession of particular bishops charged with the care of wide stretches of territory. Nor could one urge against such a conclusion the lack of an explicit apostolic command sanctioning and establishing this institution for all times and places, since it would be implicit in an apostolic mandate designed to take care of the needs of the second generation. Only those who had official authorization to propagate the office would be able to do so. This conclusion would be demanded had Christ in fact founded a particular churchly office of this kind. The chief obstacle standing in the way of such a view is that Scripture is silent concerning it. However thinkable it is that the apostles gave their pupils a command of this sort,[17] it is nevertheless an established fact that the Lord was not pleased to cause their utterances to this effect to come down to us. But we cannot ascribe the same conscience-binding and conscience-pacifying force to ancient tradition as we do to a specific word of God that comes to us. This renders all the more meaningful and important for us the derivation of St Timothy's grace of office (the χάρισμα) from the laying on of hands of the presbyterate that included Paul. 1 Tim 4:14; 2 Tim 1:6. However highly we might place the rank of an evangelist, Timothy would accordingly have received his office through the presbyterate. We should at all events have to ascribe the same effect to the presbyterate's laying on of hands as to the laying on of hands of the apostle himself. Just as in Ac 13:1ff "prophets and teachers," men of the second rung of offices, received the divine command to separate and ordain [74] apostles, that is, men of the first rung, so according to 1 Tim 4:14 a presbyterate ordained an evangelist, who in terms of rank stood above the other presbyters. Accordingly we must concede to presbyters not just the ordination of presbyters in general, but also of those presbyters who, like Timothy, carried out the governance of the Church, that is, of bishops. For the tasks of an evangelist concurred so closely with those of a bishop as to be exchangeable. Thus the presbyterate propagated itself through the presbyterate and a *presbyteral* succession—by way of contrast with the episcopal succession of later ages—is not an idea to be dismissed out of hand. Anyone who has become a presbyter through a bishop or a presbyter could be as certain as Timothy not only of his duty with God's help but also of his right to ordain and to propagate the grace and authority of the office. We would accordingly be obliged to acknowledge as legitimate ordinations by such bishops of the post-apostolic age as were orthodox or regarded as orthodox, for they were presbyters. Yet conversely our presbyteral ordination would also have to appear legitimate, for the presbyterate would have the authority to ordain—in the office itself would lie the authority to transmit it further. Presbyters could ordain a Timothy, i.e., a bishop, for themselves and others, for they would be ordaining a presbyter, whose appointing, visiting, and judging of presbyters would not exceed the presbyterate's competence in relation to its members and the congregations. And yet it would be possible, for the sake of good order and for other [75] reasons, to concede to the presbyters entrusted with the Church's governance the privilege of being the presbyterate's mouth and representative at the appointment and ordination of presbyters. This would be a human right whose estimate as a divine ordinance could be precluded by doctrine and other means. The only question would be whether the statement defended among us, that in case of necessity call without ordination would suffice for the office, may be maintained, whether consistency does not demand that ordination be placed higher than is done by many old teachers of the Lutheran Church. These teachers sometimes call ordination a solemn declaration and announcement of a call received (*solemnem declarationem vocationis*), which is certainly too little. They do not deny the grace of office outright, nor that it is given at ordination; they simply maintain that it is not given through the laying on of hands, but through the hearing of prayer. Yet the prayer is after all an ordination prayer, spoken by ordaining presbyters, and it is not claimed that the grace of office is bestowed as the hearing of other prayers offered outside the ordination. In general the Lutheran teachers find themselves with respect to ordination in an embarrassment of their own making. If ordination is nothing more than the solemn announcement of a call, namely to serve a local congregation, why is it then asserted that it cannot be repeated? But if it can be repeated, what would the difference then be between it and installation, which has quite the same form in our circles and which might possibly be bestowed on a man twenty-five times in his life? [76] We shall indeed have to concede that ordination is more and counts for more than is customarily assumed, that it gives competence and authorization for the exercise of office in a more universal way, that a charisma, a grace and gift of office comes through it, that the statement *sine titulo ne quis ordinetur* ("no one shall be ordained without having found a particular sphere of activity") must be interpreted thus: "No one shall receive the *universal authorization and gift of the office* before he can use it *somewhere*." Conversely, installation to a particular sphere of activity will present itself in such a way that it becomes a kind of development and pouring forth of ordination for particular spheres of activity, a conveyance of the stream of grace that sprang from ordination, whereby it too would cease to be a mere ceremony. Yet we are unwittingly straying onto territory onto which we did not for the moment intend to step, since we believe ourselves obliged to speak on ordination in a special chapter. In this place we should only say that the so-called episcopal succession ultimately boils down to a succession of presbyters and is nothing but a concrete expression of the principle that the divinely instituted office has the duty, right, and authorization independently to propagate itself and its graces, an authorization that is more important for the preservation of the Church than is currently demonstrated to a superficial examination.

We presume to add but one further point here. Before us lies a little writing of a presbyter of the Anglican Church, a Church against whose practice what has been [77] said to this point testifies no less than it does against that of the Roman Church. The writing has the title, *A Letter to a Methodist. By a Presbyter of the Diocese of Maryland. Baltimore 1844*. Wesley had nominated two men as superintendents of the new preacherless Methodist congregations in North America, men who subsequently became significant as bishops of the (Episcopal) Methodists. The author of the little writing now proves to the Methodist to whom he writes that, despite the names having an identical meaning, bishop and superintendent are two different things. According to him, a superintendent is a human order that the man Wesley was able to found, whereas a bishop is more, that is, a divine order competent and empowered to transmit further the gracious streams of the New Testament office, namely by appointing and ordaining bishops. Yet Wesley was only a presbyter and therefore could not make others to be what he himself was not, that is, bishops. He is alleged to have perceived his error and subsequently to have sought episcopal ordination from Anglican bishops for his superintendents. This is a striking proof if a bishop is indeed a special order, but a completely nugatory proof if he is a rung of the presbyterate, for which he needs a new pouring out of the river of grace at installation, a new flowing forth of the old ordination, but no new ordination. It is a completely nugatory proof if the Lystra presbyterate's ordination of Timothy is valid, an ordination of man who discharged episcopal tasks if anyone did. It is a completely nugatory proof if a succession not of bishops but of presbyters lies in the concept of the holy office, [78] so that a college of presbyters–in the case of necessity, just one of their number–can give to an aspirant the official authority that they themselves have in an extension and for a purpose implicit in the circumstances and required for the welfare of the Church. And yet it remains correct with respect to our superintendents and to the concept of a superintendent (or of a dean, as we say) that such a superintendent or dean is still no bishop in the sense of the first age after the apostles. We become familiar with episcopal tasks from the example of Timothy and Titus, even though these men did not yet bear the name of bishop that distinguished them from their fellow elders. In this point too the symbolic books of our Church are in complete agreement with Holy Scripture. A bishop appoints, ordains, and judges presbyters as his equals, he watches over discipline and doctrine and deposes the wicked in virtue of the divine commandments and of the office that he bears. Elected and blessed by their equals, bishops are overshepherds whose congregation is simply more extended than that of their fellow presbyters and which includes the latter themselves as sheep.

Such overshepherds for the shepherds and their congregations, such fellow elders and fellow workers are without doubt worthy of all honor and to be desired for the Church, which has a deep need for such ministry, a need that can absolutely not be met by princely and royal superintendents. The latter, their clerical status notwithstanding, are nevertheless civil servants of a secular lord, nominated by him to set in motion a certain sum of regulations of their lord (and bishop) and to watch over other people's obedience towards them. They ultimately represent more the prince, their supreme bishop, [79] than the diocese in relation to him. One could only wish that this assertion were no longer true.

> Note. It might not be incorrect to lay serious emphasis in our time on the following words. The distinction between office and congregation is scriptural. Presbyters are consecrated or ordained. Whoever is ordained to the office is no longer a layman. Hence it follows that there can be no such thing as a "lay elder" or a "lay presbyter." Either they are laymen, in which case they are not presbyters, or they are presbyters, in which case they are not laymen. Ordination makes the difference between them and the congregation (the people=the laity), a difference that no one can annul by the fully correct claim that all Christians are priests (*sacerdotes*). For the office of the New Testament and the universal priesthood of Christians are *different* things. The presbyters have and exercise the universal priesthood, but the Christians who are God's priests are not for this reason elders. Presbyterate and priesthood [*Sazerdotium*] do not coincide. Let no one confuse what the Lord distinguishes. Not fittingly keeping these two concepts apart has wrought great confusion in recent times, and what a long lament could be raised on this score!

VIII. The Deacons[8]

§28. We read in Ac 2:42 concerning the first Christian congregation [*Gemeine*] in Jerusalem [80], Ἦσαν δὲ προσκαρτεροῦντες τῇ διδαχῇ τῶν ἀποστόλων καὶ τῇ κοινωνίᾳ, τῇ κλάσει τοῦ ἄρτου καὶ ταῖς προσευχαῖς ("They continued in the apostles' teaching and in fellowship and in the breaking of bread and in prayer," as Luther translates). Simple as these words are when examined at a merely superficial level, when viewed with somewhat greater precision they actually give much food for thought. It is specifically the expression κοινωνία that provokes reflection. Κοινωνία means "fellowship." Now preaching, the breaking of bread, and common prayer are already association, fellowship. What can we then think of as a special form of fellowship that lurks under the expressly emphasized word κοινωνία? Since fellowship in spiritual goods is already alluded to in continuance in the apostles' doctrine and in the breaking of bread, and fellowship in the seeking of God and spiritual goods in continuance in prayer, consideration of κοινωνία points to a fellowship of life, inclining us to understand thereby all fellowship that is not already intimated by the apostles' doctrine, the breaking of bread, and prayer, hence every form of fellowship in love that demonstrates itself in life. We would not at all deny the correctness of this understanding. Moreover, there is in Holy Scripture yet another particular application of the word κοινωνία that gives a sharp edge to the general concept and sheds light on our passage.

Just two words after the cited passage, in v. 44[f.], the adjective κοινός (common) occurs in a sense precisely [81] connected to v. 42. We read that the believers "had all things *in common*; and they

[8] Cf. *Proposal for an Association of Lutheran Christians for Apostolic Life. Together with a Draft of a Catechism of Apostolic Life* (1848), p. 90. II. On Fellowship.

sold their possessions and goods and distributed them to all, as any had need [RSV]" (εἶχον ἅπαντα κοινά, καὶ τὰ κτήματα καὶ τὰς ὑπάρξεις ἐπίπρασκον καὶ διεμέριζον αὐτὰ πᾶσι καθότι ἄν τις χρείαν εἶχε. So far did "continuance in fellowship" go, then, that no one called anything that he possessed his own, but they had everything in common, as Ac 4:32 explains by way of repetition, illustrating this with concrete examples in v. 33ff. (Τοῦ δὲ πλήθους τῶν πιστευσάντων ἦν ἡ καρδία καὶ ἡ ψυχὴ μία· καὶ οὐδ' εἷς τι τῶν ὑπαρχόντων αὐτῷ ἔλεγεν ἴδιον εἶναι, ἀλλ' ἦν αὐτοῖς ἅπαντα κοινά., v. 32). We shall come to speak again later of this fellowship in material goods. We have to do here only with the meaning of the words κοινός, κοινωνία, κοινωνεῖν. The first thing to note is that κοινός and, on account of the connection with v. 42, κοινωνία are used of fellowship in earthly goods.

Our next encounter with the word κοινωνεῖν occurs in Rom 12:13. The apostle says how the saints are to be, and among other things he states, Ταῖς χρείαις τῶν ἁγίων κοινωνοῦντες (Luther: "Take on yourselves the need of the saints," or: "Share the needs of the saints," "Make common what is yours." ["Contribute to the needs of the saints" RSV]) We patently have here the same fellowship in earthly goods named above. Saints should acknowledge the needs of other saints as their own and seek to meet them through the sharing of temporal goods.

We see especially in Rom 15:26 how far [82] this use of language has progressed. εὐδόκησαν (it is said) Μακεδονία καὶ Ἀχαΐα κοινωνίαν τινὰ ποιήσασθαι[18] εἰς τοὺς πτωχοὺς τῶν ἁγίων τῶν ἐν Ἱερουσαλήμ. ("Those from Macedonia and Achaea have willingly contributed a common tax for the poor saints in Jerusalem"). κοινωνία is here no longer only the act of sharing, but, as in our word "collect," there is almost already a union of the concept of giving with that of *gift*. There is a completely parallel application of the word to spiritual goods in the immediately following v. 27, εὐδόκησαν γάρ, καὶ ὀφειλέται αὐτῶν εἰσιν. εἰ γὰρ τοῖς πνευματικοῖς αὐτῶν ἐκοινώνησαν τὰ ἔθνη,[19] ὀφείλουσι καὶ ἐν τοῖς σαρκικοῖς λειτουργῆσαι αὐτοῖς. ("They were pleased to do it, and indeed they are in debt to them, for if the Gentiles have come to share in their spiritual blessings, they also ought to be of service to them in material blessings [RSV].")

Of a piece with the passages just cited are also the passages that we find in Paul's glorious discourses concerning the collection taken up for the poor Jewish Christians in Judea; 2 Cor 8:4; 9:13). It is unnecessary here to furnish a further explanation of this passage also. We wish only to take the occasion of mentioning in favor of the Lutheran doctrine of the holy meal that in 1 Cor 10:16 κοινωνία is easily and beautifully explained in terms of the use of language in the related passages just listed.

The passages quoted will suffice to prove our assertion that Ac 2:42 speaks chiefly [83] of the fellowship of love in temporal things, but they will also make clear that the fellowship of love manifested itself especially through the joyful offering of earthly goods for the welfare of the brethren. In the context of the entire holy life of the first congregation we can confidently say that here is the origin of the oblations in the divine service, of the churchly works of mercy and care for the sick from which derives the whole sacred institution of the diaconate. It is admittedly not yet fully clear in Ac 2:44, 45 that a giving within the divine service is in view, but it rather seems as though those moved to mercy distributed their tender gifts themselves. Yet we find in Ac 4:32ff and 5:1ff that all gifts were laid at the apostles' feet, and the whole procedure acquires the most decisively spiritual stamp. One's charity was placed at the disposal of the presbytery, and where else might this be done than at the divine service where one also had the apostles' doctrine, the breaking of bread, and the prayers (Ac 2:42)? Churchly giving and oblations furnished the occasion for the holy ecclesial office of the diaconate or of the care of the poor. The κοινωνία or fellowship of which we speak is one of the most glorious ideas of the New Testament which, as we shall see later, is often put forth with enthusiasm by St Paul. And just as κοινωνία is used in the sense of all kinds of sharing, from the most cerebral to the most material, such as was the collection for the poor, so we find a corresponding range in the concept of διακονία or *diakonia*, which is used from the lofty heights of the service of the holy office right down to the level of the delivery of a collection and even of the concept of a *collection* itself. Simply compare Ac [84] 11:29; 12:25; Rom 12:7; 15:25. Nevertheless we now wish to subject the office of *diakonia*, the glorious bearer of Christendom's holy κοινωνία, to closer examination in its original and its relationships. We shall delight in the office that is so richly discussed in Holy Scripture, that was glorified by the first martyr, and that dripped with so much blessing in the history of the Christian Church! Yet we shall also lament how this office has declined and how its sphere of operation has come to be placed in other hands! The big need of our own time is resurrection[9] of the *sacred diakonia* of Christians. The least effect of its restoration would be the disappearance of proletarians from Christian congregations! But before διακονία comes κοινωνία, whose office it is, and before this holy sacrificial brotherly love, and before this the love of Jesus, which is lacking.

§29. Holy Scripture does not relate the emergence of the presbyterate on its territory distinct from that of the apostolate or of the office of evangelist. On the one hand, there were too many telling analogies in Judaism and, on the other, having presiding officers is too much a natural feature of every emerging society to warrant much mention of the origin and introduction of the Christian office that was meant [85] to satisfy the congregation's need for leadership. Conversely fellowship, κοινωνία, and its office, διακονία, the diaconate, is something new and proper to Christianity, something in which the new spirit of the new, single body of Christ, the spirit of love, is most beautifully expressed.

9   This would at all events involve more than the admittedly highly noteworthy suggestion, taken from the sphere of temporal life, to cultivate and enhance the guilds of the Germans. See (Marbach's) *Open Letter to all Guild Members of Germany and at the same time to all Citizens and Fathers of Households. On 22 Guilds at Leipzig.* 1848.

This is why immediate mention is made and, as we clearly see, a careful description given of the emergence of this new institution.

The Christians at Jerusalem brought the gifts of their love and deposited them (Ac 4:32, 34, 35, 37; 5:2) at the feet of the apostles; thus the apostles administered them. This added such a burden to the daily work of the apostles, however, that it was not possible for them fully to cope with it. In Ac 6:1 therefore there arises a murmuring of the Hellenists, that is, of the Greek-speaking Jewish Christians, against the Hebrews, because their widows were being overlooked in the daily *service* (ὅτι παρεθεωροῦντο ἐν τῇ διακονίᾳ τῇ καθημερινῇ αἱ χῆραι αὐτῶν). The Twelve thereupon gathered "the multitude of the disciples" (τὸ πλῆθος τῶν μαθητῶν) and explained that it was by no means fitting (ἀρεστόν) for them to leave the Word of God and wait upon tables (διακονεῖν τραπέζαις). "'Therefore, brethren,' they said, 'pick out from among you seven men of good repute, full of the Spirit and of wisdom, whom we may appoint to this duty. But we will devote ourselves to prayer and the ministry of the word (διακονίᾳ τοῦ λόγου).' And what they said pleased the whole multitude, and they chose Stephen, a man full of faith and of the Holy Spirit, and Philip, and Prochorus, and Nicanor, and [86] Timon, and Parmenas, and Nicolaus, a proselyte of Antioch. These they set before the apostles, and they prayed and laid their hands upon them" [RSV] (ἐπισκέψασθε δὲ ἀδελφοί, ἄνδρας ἐξ ὑμῶν μαρτυρουμένους ἑπτά, πλήρεις Πνεύματος καὶ σοφίας, οὓς καταστήσομεν ἐπὶ τῆς χρείας ταύτης. ἡμεῖς δὲ τῇ προσευχῇ καὶ τῇ διακονίᾳ τοῦ λόγου προσκαρτερήσομεν. καὶ ἤρεσεν ὁ λόγος ἐνώπιον παντὸς τοῦ πλήθους καὶ ἐξελέξαντο Στέφανον, ἄνδρα πλήρης πίστεως καὶ πνεύματος ἁγίου, καὶ [Φίλιππον καὶ Πρόχορον καὶ Νικάνορα καὶ Τίμωνα καὶ Παρμενᾶν καὶ Νικόλαον προσήλυτον Ἀντιοχέα,] οὓς ἔστησαν ἐνώπιον τῶν ἀποστόλων· καὶ προσευξάμενοι ἐπέθηκαν αὐτοῖς τὰς χεῖρας).

Note the great difference between the nomination of deacons and the appointment of presbyters! The "multitude of believers," the congregation, is not called in for the latter, which lies completely in the hands of the appointing apostles and evangelists, who involve the congregation and its members according to their judgment and according to the need of the situation. Conversely, the multitude is called together for the introduction of the diaconate, the plan is laid before it–albeit in the imperative, for the apostles are the Lord's representatives–, it gives and expresses its approval. And how are the deacons produced? According to the norm of necessary qualities determined by the apostles, they are *elected by the congregation*, presented to the apostles, and ordained by them. We might call the presbyterate a sacred aristocracy in the Church, while something democratic lies in the election of deacons. An aristocratic and a democratic element of the original church polity steps before our eyes. The presbyterate, which the apostles themselves superbly [87] describe as a διαμονία τῆς προσευχῆς καί τοῦ λόγου, brings the Lord's mandate and His holy shepherding love to the congregation. Conversely, the diaconate administers the voluntary alms of the congregation for the benefit of the congregation's members, it is an office of the congregation over the treasures of the congregation. Where the Lord's office is to be propagated, the servants selected by the Lord are in charge, the bearers of His office, according to their competence and their divine authority. Where the most sacred activation of the congregation's mercy requires an office, the congregation may cooperate through its election, which is one of the many proofs how much the liberated good will of the congregation is honoured in Holy Scripture. Yet both offices, presbyterate and diaconate, stand in the most beautiful relationship. The administrators of their gifts of love elected by the congregation do not stand against the presbyterate, as though it were needful to represent the rights of the flock against the holy pastoral office. The pastoral office is over all, even over the deacons. The diaconate branches off from the presbyterate of the apostles, who in their capacity as the first presbyters were the first welfare officers of the congregations. The diaconate stems from the presbyterate and stands under the presbyterate. Indeed, the newly elected deacons are presented to the presbyterate and ordained by it. And the presbyters stand in a supervisory, participatory capacity over the deacons and their office even after their ordination and induction. We have a clear testimony of this in Ac 11:30. Not the deacons but the διδάσκαλοι [teachers] of Antioch bring the collection for the poor Jewish Christians to Jerusalem, and not the deacons but the presbyters [88] of the congregation of Jerusalem receive the Antiochene gifts, obviously not in order to distribute them but in order to deliver them over to the deacons so that they might administer them in keeping with their own office.

What a wise institution of God is this diaconate! The congregation fears nothing from the deacons, for it elected them according to its trust; and the presbyters fear nothing from them, for they blessed and instituted them, albeit having examined them (according to the principles expressed in 1 Tim 3) prior to the blessing and appointment. The office is not one with the presbyterate, for it branched off from it. There's an end to disbursing the Church's goods according to the interests of the presbyters alone: the deacons elected by the congregation watch over these goods. Nor are these goods administered according to worldly notions, for the deacons are ordained, blessed by the presbyterate, a churchly college closely united to the presbyterate, subordinate to it as is the body to the soul. Just like κοινωνία, fellowship, so διακονία, the care of the poor, proceeded from the sanctuary of God, from the tenderest love. Everything is holy, everything is churchly in the sequence: the poor [person], the gifts for him, the administration of the gifts, the carers for the poor. This is the spirit of Christianity, the Spirit of the Lord Jesus! Here we see holy aristocracy and holy democracy united in the work of mercy! Where things are thus, the State is spared the work. Where the Church has and does her office, there what is possible for the relief of temporal misery takes place in the most beautiful way. Here is in my opinion the great *pium desiderium*[20] of the present time, which is [89] by no means fulfilled by the caricature of setting up the male and female diaconate that we have experienced.

§30. We can ascertain the deacons' *range of duties* from what prompted the emergence of their office. The congregation's gifts of love handed over to the presbyterate were distributed to the needy by the deacons. They took over the daily distribution (διακονία καθημερινή) for which the apostles had no time. In the congregation at Jerusalem this office preeminently took the form of a "serving at tables." The widows and other poor people ate together, and the deacons saw to it that each received their portion. Yet it goes without saying that food was not the only need of the poor that the collected funds were intended to alleviate. They needed clothing, for example, they needed many things in order to cope with their distresses. These things had also to be included in the daily distribution. Matters were structured differently in other congregations, where the poor did not actually eat together, so that *diakonia* could lose the character of serving at tables and yet, as we actually discover in what follows, there could still be a concern for the daily distribution. We can therefore say in general that *diakonia* is care for the poor in the sense and spirit of the Church, and yet we cannot call it care for the sick in such a general sense. The better-off families looked after their own sick, so that only the care of sick poor folk fell into *diakonia*'s domain because the sick poor stood in need of the daily distribution just as much as and even more than the healthy poor. We therefore do not need to explain *diakonia* as the care of both the poor and the sick, [90] but can abide with its being a care of the poor that encompassed the poor of all kinds, children and widows, the healthy and the sick, the living and the dying. Understand this sphere of activity solely in the sense of Christian love and you will indeed find it sufficiently wide and rich not to need filling up with alien tasks. When Ac 6:3 determines that the carers of the poor must be "full of the Holy Spirit and of wisdom," we are not obliged to surmise that they were invested with such official functions as belonged more in the range of the presbyters' tasks, such as, for example, that teaching and preaching pertained to them on account of their office. As deacons they had only the care of the sick and this office is already such as to require Spirit and wisdom in and for itself. Do not refute this statement by pointing to Stephen and Philip. Stephen performed miracles, which others in the congregation also performed who were neither presbyters nor deacons nor prophets etc. Stephen's miracles drew attention and the enemies began to dispute with him (συζητεῖν), Ac 6:9, and yet disputing is neither teaching nor preaching, but–especially bearing Jewish customs in mind–it fell to everyone who had the desire and the gift for it. Stephen's speech before the sacred council was not a sermon but a speech of defense for which the Lord had promised "mouth and wisdom" to each of His persecuted ones. Stephen's speech is a powerful discourse that mounts to the level of a prophetic word and finally to that of a prophetic vision, but it was not a sermon, and much less may we draw from it the conclusion that a teaching office pertained to the deacons *as such*. [91] Reference to Philip's great volume of teaching activity seems more convincing, and yet it is not. For Philip taught when the congregation of Jerusalem was scattered and its deacons with it, when the office of *diakonia* was ripped from its congregation. *Diakonia* binds to place and congregation. That Philip neither baptized nor taught qua *deacon* is demonstrated by the simple fact that he was an *evangelist*, Ac 21:8. The evangelist travels, while the deacon is resident somewhere; the evangelist preaches and baptizes, while the deacon looks after his sick. These are very different offices, and they should have been blended just as little in subsequent epochs as they were in the first congregation. Once the process had begun of conferring official clerical tasks on deacons as such, it intensified to the point that *diakonia* ceased to be care of the poor and turned into a clerical auxiliary office that encroached on the presbyterate, until at last Christians' sacred care of the poor completely disappeared and the care of the poor became in recent times a matter for the State. Let us hold fast from the New Testament to *diakonia*'s being care of the poor and *as such a sacred office of the Church*.

§31. We find in 1 Tim 3:8 the *prerequisites* for the diaconate prescribed by the apostle Paul. They should first be tested in line with these prerequisites and then serve (Οὗτοι δὲ δοκιμαζέσθωσαν πρῶτον, εἶτα διακονείτωσαν ἀνέγκλητοι ὄντες, v. 10). When discussing the presbyters we did not take a closer look at these prerequisites and we intend also here to refrain from this endeavor. Besides, every word is crystal clear, even though [92] two of them, that are used in equal measure of both the presbyter and the deacon, stand in need of special explanation. We mean, first, αἰσχροκερδὴς [blameless RSV; of unimpeachable character NEB] (1 Tim 3:3, 8; Tit 1:7), and, secondly, μιᾶς γυναικὸς ἄνδρα [husband of one wife] (1 Tim 3:2, 12; Tit 1:6), which last requirement also recurs in corresponding form for the widows in 1 Tim 5:9 (ἑνὸς ἀνδρὸς γυνὴ). Some reservation attaches to the word αἰσχροκερδὴς in virtue of Luther's translation "not pursuing any dishonorable line of business" [*nicht unehrliche Hantierung treiben*], whereas the word surely refers to each and every shameful way of acquiring gain for oneself, and the question what kind of business a presbyter and deacon may or may not pursue on the side lies further from the word αἰσχροκερδὴς than seems to be the case when we read Luther's translation.

§32. *Deacon's wives* are given special consideration in 1 Tim 3:11, although the writer's meaning may encompass not only deacons' wives but also the wives of presbyters, who have been spoken of three verses previously. Entirely distinct from deacons' wives are *female deacons* or, as they were later called, deaconesses. Such a deaconess was the Phoebe commended to the Romans by St Paul in Rom 16:1 (Συνίστημι δὲ ὑμῖν Φοίβην τὴν ἀδελφὴν ἡμῶν, οὖσαν διάκονον τῆς ἐκκλησίας τῆς ἐν Κεγχρεαῖς, ἵνα αὐτὴν προσδέξησθε ἐν κυρίῳ ἀξίως τῶν ἁγίων καὶ παραστῆτε αὐτῇ ἐν ᾧ ἂν ὑμῶν χρῄζῃ πράγματι· καὶ γὰρ αὐτὴ προστάτις πολλῶν ἐγενήθη καὶ αὐτοῦ ἐμοῦ.). Apparently also belonging to the same female office of service were the women to whom the apostle ascribes a [93] κοπιᾶν ἐν κυρίῳ, a laboring to the point of exhaustion in the Lord,[10] e.g., Mary in Rom 16:6 (Ἀσπάσασθε Μαριάμ, ἥτις πολλὰ ἐκοπίασεν εἰς ἡμᾶς), and Tryphaena, Tryphosa, and Persis in Rom 16:12 (Ἀσπάσασθε Τρύφαιναν καὶ Τρυφῶσαν τὰς κοπιώσας ἐν κυρίῳ. Ἀσπάσασθε Περσίδα τὴν ἀγαπητήν, ἥτις πολλὰ ἐκοπίασεν ἐν κυρίῳ). This distinction between the wives of church servants and female church servants might help call those to order who in their overflowing goodness these days wish to apply to pastors' wives the office and indeed even the title of deaconesses. Married women are unfitted to the office of deaconess right from the word go. Their concern is with their husbands' house and family. It is honor enough that they find special mention and proof of the high regard paid to their position. Deaconesses must be free of all that, they were *widows* and later virgins.

Ac 6:1[11] already mentions *widows* [94] who had been overlooked in the daily distribution and who were therefore poor widows. In 1 Tim 5:3ff we read again of widows, but, as the whole context makes clear, not precisely of widows who are simply the objects of care, but of those who, as the congregation furnished them with means of support, could also be used to provide care for other poor people. We can deduce from the verse 1 Tim 5:16 that such widows found support in the congregation: "If a Christian man or woman has widows in the family, he must support them himself;

---

10 Cf. 1 Cor 6:16. This verse speaks of the household of Stephanas, which, after being the firstfruits of the kingdom of God in Achaea, devoted itself to the service of the saints (εἰς διακονίαν τοῖς ἁγίοις ἔταξαν ἑαυτούς). Paul urges subjection to them and to everyone who labors and toils with them (παντὶ τῷ συνεργοῦντι καὶ κοπιῶντι).
11 Cf Ac 9:39 on the death of Tabitha. "...they took [Peter] to the upper room. All the widows stood beside him weeping, and showing coats and garments which Dorcas made while she was with them" (Καὶ παρέστησαν αὐτῷ πᾶσαι αἱ χῆραι κλαίουσαι καὶ ἐπιδεικνύμεναι χιτῶνας καὶ ἱμάτια ὅσα ἐποίει μετ' αὐτῶν οὖσα ἡ Δορκάς).

the congregation must be relieved of the burden, so that it may be free to support those who are widows in the full sense of the term" [NEB] (Εἴ τις πιστὴ ἔχει χήρας, ἐπαρκείτω αὐταῖς καὶ μὴ βαρείσθω ἡ ἐκκλησία, ἵνα ταῖς ὄντως χήραις ἐπαρκέσῃ, vs. 16). That they were also used for the service of the congregation we easily find by paying careful attention to several words in vv 3ff that can only be understood on the basis of such a presupposition. (Vs 4, a widow who has children or grandchildren shall first learn τὸν ἴδιον οἶκον εὐσεβεῖν—Bengel: *familiam pie tractare*, Luther: "divinely rule" her own house—*before she wants to serve the Church in her poor members etc. etc.)*

What employment the apostle had in mind for these deaconesses can be established on the basis of what has been adduced from his mouth above. It was *care of the poor*, which embraced the care of the poor, orphans, widows, and sick of the female sex and surely also of those male poor or sick who stood in special need of female hands. [95] Therefore no widow under sixty years could be chosen (Χήρα καταλεγέσθω μὴ ἔλαττον ἐτῶν ἑξήκοντα γεγονυῖα, v 9). That these widows could not be used for any kind of public teaching activity in the Church proceeds from Paul's universal rule according to which public speaking was not permitted to any woman, 1 Tim 2:12; 1 Cor 14:34. Conversely, as also in the case of the male deacons, several forms of external assistance in the divine service could be attached to the deaconesses' office. At female baptisms, for example, the service of female deacons was greatly to be desired and indeed veritably mandated by considerations of decency. And yet Scripture is silent on this topic, and it is our intention here to set forth only scriptural content.

§33. In the *Proposal for the Union of Lutheran Christians for Apostolic Living* p. 84ff, § 36, we have spoken of the obedience that the congregation owes the holy office by apostolic command. We showed there on p. 88f that this obedience is commanded also towards the deacons. This injunction raises the office of *diakonia* in our eyes. We refer to those pages. We do not wish to speak long on the passage 1 Tim 3:13 where faithful deacons are promised that through their administration of office they shall gain a *beautiful rung* [good standing RSV]. Whether progress here or a special degree of glory hereafter is meant, it is enough that the diaconate has a special promise from which it can take comfort. [96] If only a rung or step towards the higher church office of the presbyterate is meant, it could still not be denied that this promise gives the deacons powerful encouragement to persevere in their zeal. It also serves to elevate the presbyterate, and that by the mouth of an apostle, so that it would not be vanity to struggle to attain this rank. For St Paul also speaks elsewhere, "If anyone aspires to the office of bishop, he desires a noble task" [precious work: Luther] (1 Tim 3:1 RSV). If the Lord attached the least reward to faithful *diakonia*, His act and speech would make it great, a truth that holds all the more firmly when it applies to something sufficiently high and good, as is the bishop's office in and for itself.

§34. But something else might be worthy of further mention here. Each congregation had its care of the poor and the sacred foundation of the diaconate was instituted by the Lord for this local office. But just as the Christians of one and the same local congregation acknowledged it as their sacred duty to see to it that there were no poor among them (Οὐδὲ γὰρ ἐνδεής τις ἦν ἐν αὐτοῖς, Ac 4:34), so likewise the various congregations, no matter how far they might be separated from each other, acknowledged it as a sacred duty to meet each others' needs. *Diakonia* therefore extended over the whole Church. And what a wealth of carers for the poor did this entail! When it was imperative to take a contribution to the Jewish Christians, the apostle Paul, a lofty apostle, considers it worth the effort himself to travel to Jerusalem in order to bring from faraway lands gifts and offerings for the Jewish Christians; Rom 15:25. (Νυνὶ δὲ πορεύομαι εἰς Ἰερουσαλὴμ διακονῶν τοῖς ἁγίοις). [97] And not just this. Deputations from the congregations, "apostles of the churches" (2 Cor 8:23),[12] must accompany him

---

12 Titus, Luke, through whose hands, at any rate according to the signature of the letter, the second epistle reached the Corinthians.

when he brings up a contribution, as we read with joyful attention in 2 Cor 8:16ff. Thus the congregations do not simply give, but care is taken that the giving takes place and that the gift is brought in a glorious, worthy, and solemn way, with prayer and thanks to God. All congregations [*Gemeinen*] exercise mutual fellowship, κοινωνία, and all servants of Christ from apostle down to deacon are deacons, are zealous and active in the care of the poor, and those who carry on their lips the word of life that makes eternally rich bring in their hands the offerings of congregations far and wide for the relief of earthly misery. *Diakonia* writ large, a bond of union, of connection, of remembrance, and of love! Let this not be said in vain! What enthused apostles should also enthuse us. If we know these things, blessed are we if we do them!

IX. Concerning Ordination

§35. In § 23 we attributed the appointment of presbyters to the presbytery and claimed that none of the examples preserved in Scripture indicate the people's participating in a leading role. [98] And in §27 we made the further claim that the office is propagated by those who have it. Yet in the process we dared to contradict our great Lutheran dogmaticians who allege proof not only from the custom of the early Church, the decretals of the popes, and statements of the Fathers (See John Gerhard, *Loci Theologici* XII, p. 96 ff. §94ff.) but also from Holy Scripture (Gerhard, *op.cit.*, p. 85ff., §87ff.), that a share, indeed a very significant share in the election [of presbyters] belongs to the congregation, and even that both ordination and election take place through the ministers in the name of the congregation (*op.cit.*, p. 159, §154). It could well be that closer inspection of, for example, the passages from the Church Fathers etc. adduced by Gerhard would not prove precisely what Gerhard would like to see them prove, namely, a formal χειροτονία and election by the congregation, and thus that these passages would themselves lend support to the congregation's share in the election being as stated in §23. Be this as it may, it seems certain that our dear fathers read into these *Scripture passages* too much of the custom of their own day along with a defense of it. They wanted to involve all "three estates" of the Church, presbytery, rulers, and congregation, in the election in order to justify the influence exercised by the princes and, in the cities, by the congregations. Alas, the longer they did so, the more they paid homage to the territorial system in its various developments; and since the New Testament offers no clear evidence in its favour, more obscure passages (obscure at any rate [99] with respect to the interpretations made of them) and the rights of the theocratic kings of the Old Covenant were obliged to supply as much assistance as possible.

On such a reading, the passages Ac 1:23ff.; 13:2ff.; 14:23ff. attest the right of congregations in the election of shepherds and teachers. We find a compact summary of this point of view in Quenstedt (p. 131f.)

Yet whether they may yield much or little for the issue, two of the passages listed must remain entirely outside of consideration, Ac 1:23ff concerning the election of the apostle Matthias and Ac 6:3ff concerning the election of the deacons. To be sure, at the election of the apostle Matthias around 120 disciples were present, St Peter's speech addresses them and ἔστησαν δύο (vs. 23) and προσευξάμενοι εἶπαν [vs. 24] can easily be referred to the entire number of those present. And yet it might also be the case that, as at the apostolic council in Ac 15, the disciples present stood supportively at the apostles' side, quietly or loudly approved the steps taken, and helped to pray, without playing an active role in the election. Nothing is said to the effect that the apostles had commanded something with respect to the mode of the election and the participation of the congregation, nor even that the congregation did anything conspicuous in the process. Moreover, it was an *apostle* who was to be elected. On account of the requirements stated by Peter, the election was conducted within very narrow and therefore simple parameters. Moreover, the election in itself was not completely decisive inasmuch as the final choice fell to the Lord, who accomplished it [100] by means of the lot and went on at Pentecost to ordain the one elected in a manner that showed the lot itself to have been the instrument of His providence. Moreover, the story of the outpouring of the Holy Spirit is told in such close connection to the election of the apostle Matthias that one must think that the apostles, on whom the Spirit was to come, had to be numerically at full strength again before He came. The case is, then, an extraordinary one, and the participation of the congregation (which is anyway the lesser factor) is sketched in such vague terms, that no one has a right to draw conclusions for the election of presbyters from the election of Matthias. It might therefore be utterly inappropriate to conclude, as did our fathers (both here and in Ac 13:2ff), "If the congregation shared in such a way in the election for extraordinary offices, how much more should and must it do so in the case of the ordinary offices." Even if the premise were correct, the conclusion can be contested. The most intimate connection and the most complete collaboration must be deemed natural in the case of a small congregation of 120 men, whose entire situation as church is analogous to the embryonic stage of human development, and who are keenly awaiting further regulations concerning their common life. It would cause surprise if the apostles had gone into closed session for the election of Matthias, especially since they had to elect someone from outside their ranks and the election could take place with the least envy and offense and with the greatest authority only in the presence and with the assistance of the entire company. And the qualifications for a replacement were so clear that they could be set before everybody's judgment. This is not to deny [101] that similar circumstances can sometimes occur in the small circle of a presbyter that render the cooperation of the people easier and more important. And yet this election of an apostle remains something quite unique that simply cannot be equated with the election of a presbyter, even if the two scenarios do have some things in common.

Nor does the second passage, Ac 6, fit into the desired pattern. Deacons and presbyters are two different things, and we have already said that the election of the deacons by the congregation and indeed only by the congregation without any franchise of the apostles and yet according to apostolic norms is to be explained in terms of the essence of this office and belongs to this essence. The way deacons were elected can yield no evidence in support of the election of presbyters by the congregation.

With respect to the election of the apostles Barnabas and Paul in Ac 13:1ff we do not comprehend how Quenstedt can say, e.g., *op.cit.*, p. 132, "And the whole Church, which fasted and prayed, laid hands on them and sent them forth by the teachers, [and] was present–*Totaque ecclesia, quae jejunavit et oravit, per doctores manus eis imposuit et illos dimisit, praesens erat.*"At all events the first verse Ἦσαν δὲ ἐν Ἀντιοχείᾳ κατὰ τὴν οὖσαν ἐκκλησίαν προφῆται καὶ διδάσκαλοι does not intend to say that these prophets and teachers were present at a *congregational meeting*. The desire to translate Κατὰ τὴν οὖσαν ἐκκλησίαν as "at a congregational meeting" is thwarted both by τὴν οὖσαν and by the use of the word ἐκκλησία. Should one nevertheless persist with the translation "*in ecclesia,*" it can only mean, as we would say, that there were prophets and teachers "*at* that congregation." Even if the words did have the meaning that we contest [102] (which to our best knowledge no one has ever maintained), the Λειτουργούντων δὲ αὐτῶν (v. 2) and the νηστεύσαντες καὶ προσευξάμενοι and the ἀπέλυσαν could only be related to the ἐπιθέντες τὰς χεῖρας, and Quenstedt's interpretation "The Church laid on [hands] through the teachers–*ecclesia per doctores imposuit*" remains a forced exposition not justified by the way the story is told. It is, by the way, a matter of complete indifference whether one wants to refer the Λειτουργούντων to a public divine service (in keeping with the exposition of κατὰ τὴν οὖσαν ἐκκλησίαν) or, as Olshausen interprets it, to a smaller ascetic gathering staged only among the prophets and teachers. At all events not a word is said about the congregation taking part in the election or ordination of Paul and Barnabas. Therefore only the passage Ac 14:23 remains. If it says nothing, then none of the passages cited say anything about a participation of the congregation in the election of presbyters, which is the topic of this verse. Everything rests on the word χειροτονήσαντες. As they quote other, older and newer exegetes (such as Calvin, Beza, Erasmus etc.) on this passage, Quenstedt, *op.cit.*, p. 132, Gerhard, *op.cit.*, p. 94f. §93, and Calov in the *Biblia Illustrata* make every effort to take this word χειροτονεῖν, which only occurs on one other occasion in the New Testament (2 Cor 8:19, where its sense is quite unmistakable) in the sense of "elect through the votes *of others*" or "*arrange for* election." Yet not only in 2 Cor 8:19 but also in secular writers it has the sense of "elect by one's own vote, cast *one's own* franchise." It would come across as very forced and as acting for the sake of an already formed opinion if we [103] would follow the Lutheran Fathers on this point and abandon the simple meaning of a word purely in order to demonstrate that congregational participation in the election of presbyters occurs by divine right. The Syrians and Arabians have simply: *Constituerunt ac fecerunt illis seniores*; Oecumenius: Μετὰ νηστειῶν καὶ εὐχῶν ἐποίουν οἱ μαθηταί χειροτονίας. Cajetan: *Cum constituissent, hoc est, deligissent presbyteros.* This is how Gerhard himself reports the data on p. 95. And on the basis of the use of the word Olshausen argues that the apostles were in charge of the process, saying on p. 705 that, "The expression does not allow us to think of a free election on the part of the congregation, but it rather appears as though the apostles themselves sought out those suited for offices in the Church. The ethos of the community may still have been so undeveloped that this task could not have been left to the young churches. The number of those eligible for election may often have been so few that those who alone could be entrusted with offices in the Church stood forth almost automatically."

According to these remarks we shall surely be obliged to stay with what was said above in §23, and the καταστήσῃς of Tit 1:5 strengthens our resolve. The prescriptions in 1 Tim 3 and Tit 1 leave sufficient room for congregations to give their testimony and express their will, and prudent visitors–or whatever one wants to call the men who appoint presbyters–will undoubtedly have taken the wishes of the congregations into consideration as much as possible. Yet the καταστῆσαι or definitive appointment of presbyters or bishops nevertheless remains the proper preserve of the just-named officers and not that of either the people or the emperor or princes [104], who in these things belonged to the congregation. If later on, as Gerhard, for example, demonstrates (Loci XII, p. 98 §94f), congregational participation developed in a particular form, the actual καταστῆσαι remained the business of the ministerium, and when the Protestants divided the right of appointment between princes, congregations, and ministerium according to the precedent of ancient times, this occurred *jure humano* [by human right] and still lacks the requisite strict proof. Let the people retain what the Lord permitted it and what was practised in the most ancient epoch. Let us rejoice when pious congregations take an interest in the filling of ecclesiastical offices, but let no *democratic* element be introduced where none originally existed. If the passages of the fathers are read aright, we shall find that they adhered rather clearly to the pattern discernible in Holy Scripture: faithful consideration of the wishes expressed by the congregations, but also recognition of the office given to the presbytery (see 1Tim 4:14) to appoint presbyters within the geographical area of its competence. If this factor precludes violations of Scripture in the matter of filling offices, it does the same for ordination, where such violation could only result from error in the locus of how offices are to be filled. Inasmuch as ordination is conferral of office and consecration into the holy office, it is a matter for the presbytery and occurs in the name of the Lord and under His invocation, with the most intimate participation of the congregation, to which everything belongs, also the office that Christ founded.

36. Ordination is completely distinct from election and from everything that precedes election by way of inquiry into the competence and proficiency of the candidate. With respect to [105] the concept of this sacred action thoroughgoing agreement marks the explanations of the Lutheran teachers. While Balduin in the *Brevis institutio ministrorum verbi*, p. 61, ch. 8, simply calls it *vocationis confirmatio et solemnis quaedam declaratio et ministri inauguratio* [confirmation of calling, and a certain solemn declaration, and inauguration of the minister], we find a much richer definition from Hülsemann in his treatise *de ministro ordinationis sacerdot.* §1. As quoted by Quenstedt, *op.cit.*, p. 131, it reads: "Ordination is that sacred commission and action by which–in

church with the people being present, and with presbyters and deacons also being present and praying with him–the bishop or superintendent invested with ecclesiastical order and jurisdiction invests by words and the laying on of hands the presented and examined candidate for the ministry with the office of preaching the word of God and administering the sacraments in the Church, and of binding and loosing, with the accepted stipulation of obeying the rules demanded by the bishop or superintendent himself in the rite of ordination." In complete agreement with this statement is the definition that we find in Gerhard, *Loci Theologici* XII, p. 145 §139. Whether more verbosely or more concisely, they all say the same thing: ordination is conferral of office and consecration into it.

In contrast to this understanding the Romans do not find in ordination "bestowal of the office itself and still less solemn appointment to an office already bestowed," but rather "a solemn consecration whereby the one elected receives the extraordinary gifts necessary for the sacred performance of the office to which he is called." (See [Ferdinand] Walter [1794-1879], *Lehrbuch des Kirchenrechts*, 5th ed., 1831, p. 384, §210).

The full truth might perhaps lie in the middle. Since no one should be ordained without a preceding call, [106] but everyone receives ordination *in the first instance* with respect to his discharge of the office in a particular congregation, the Roman side will be unable to deny that a solemn announcement of a received call is involved in ordination. And since they themselves teach, in consequence of the passages 1 Tim 4:14 & 2 Tim 1:6,, a χάρισμα of office, a grace and gift of office (see, e.g., Balduin, *op.cit.*, 74ff.), and derive the same from ordination, the Protestants [*Evangelischen*] for their part can easily concede the efficacy of ordination and take a communication of energies [*Kräfte*] for the holy office into their definition.[13] They are right when they ascribe this endowment not to the laying on of hands in itself but to

13 "We do not deny that ordination bestows and increases the gifts of the Holy Spirit necessary for accomplishing the tasks of the ecclesiastical ministry." Gerhard, *op.cit.*, p. 168 §165.

prayer, but they will have to admit that the prayer is an ordination prayer and thus, with respect to its power and its being heard, very different from a prayer of the same content (to the extent that such a generalization can be conceded) uttered in different contexts. Whoever prays the ordination prayer is heard according to the Lord's promise, and what is expressed in the laying on of hands is a certainty of being heard that rises to the idea of an actual [simultaneous] bestowal. Gerhard expressly speaks (*op. cit.*, p. 168, §165) of a "grace of ordination" [*gratia ordinationis*]. We may not therefore sever from ordination an impartation of grace and gift such as is necessary for the office. An unprejudiced observer can indeed easily [107] find from the biblical texts that the twin factors of conferral of both office and grace of office meet in ordination.

As we consider individual passages, we must first make a distinction. Ac 13:2 and 14:23 do indeed speak of ordination and not just of a call, whereas Ac 1:23-26 says nothing about ordination but treats only a call. In Holy Scripture ordination generally has its fixed terminology [*stehende Bezeichnung*], which derives from the act that marks it, so that it is called the *laying on of hands*. Instead of "ordain" we find the expression "laying on of hands," as a review of Ac 6:6; 13:3; 14:23 and 1 Tim 4:14 and 5:22 convincingly makes plain. But at the election of Matthias no mention is made of the laying on of hands. At Pentecost the Lord laid *His* fiery hand upon him. Things stand otherwise in Ac 13:3. There Paul and Barnabas, who are expressly named apostles in Ac 14:14, are not merely called, but also ordained, and one might surmise from their ordination by human hands that they were allocated but a lower rank [*Stufe*] of the apostolate. But a more precise consideration of the passage Ac 13:3 produces a different result. Matthias' ordination was reserved for Pentecost, but Pentecost lay in the past when Paul and Barnabas were ordained. Nor was the Lord's intervention in the ordination of Paul and Barnabas in principle any less immediate and extraordinary than in the election of Matthias. The setting apart of the two occurred at the express command of the Lord, the Holy Spirit, as we see in Ac 13:2, and the ordination took place through [108] *prophets* specified by name, that is, through emissaries immediately inspired by God, which can be said of no other ordination known to us. Therefore, despite the ordination of Paul and Barnabas, the statement stands that apostles are ordained by the Lord. And it is reinforced when we bear in mind the story of Paul's conversion and the circumstance that he was raptured into the third heaven and heard words that cannot be uttered, which undoubtedly made up for the teaching by mouth that the other apostles had from the Lord during His earthly life, and which stood in relation to the great work of his life and his call to the apostolate. We might say that, alongside his ordination on earth, St Paul experienced a second ordination in heaven, that he was ordained in heaven as on earth.

Now if ordination consisted in the laying on of hands with prayers for the ordinand, after a preceding fast, we must marvel that, according to Ac 13, 14, and 6 respectively, apostles, presbyters, and deacons were ordained in completely identical fashion. If, as has already been said, the apostles belong anyway to the presbyterate in general, yet precisely in Ac 13:2 the specific distinction of this rung [*Stufe*] of the presbyterate called apostolate from the other rungs [*Stufen*] emerges with especial clarity before our eyes. In Ac 13 therefore apostolic ordination appears different from presbyteral ordination, the latter distinct from the former, and diaconal ordination different from both. Ordination is admittedly imparted in a formally identical way for different offices (the content of the ordination prayer itself certainly being different in each case), but each office still has its own [109] ordination, indeed, the apostolate, a rung [*Stufe*] of the presbyterate, has its own ordination. Further spheres of authority [*Befugnisse*] are given through a new ordination. The deacon, the presbyter, and the apostle have different spheres and levels of competence [*Befugnisse*], and therefore they have an ordination that, while admittedly formally the same, is, however, different in content. When a deacon has acquired a "beautiful rung" (βαθμὸν καλόν, 1 Tim 3:13 ["good standing" RSV]) for himself by faithful service, he can become a presbyter and receive a new ordination, and if in Ac 13 Paul and Barnabas were already προφῆται καὶ διδάσκαλοι and as διδάσκαλοι with the greatest likelihood also presbyters of the Antiochene congregation, they still require a new ordination at their promotion to the apostolate.

The Lutheran Church is quite right to hold to a single ordination. For she does not have deacons, nor will she receive any commission to ordain apostles. She has only the office of the pure presbyterate, and therefore only a single ordination, as only a single office. When she speaks of appointing "deacons," it is well known that these are no New Testament deacons or carers for the poor, but rather presbyters who align themselves under a *primus inter pares* [first among equals], as did the presbyters of old under their *primus*, the bishop. Yet if the Church should reestablish the diaconate, she would also acquire a second ordination, which, though formally similar to presbyteral ordination, would be different in virtue of the ordination prayer and therefore also in virtue of the meaning and effect of the laying on of hands and of the whole rite [*Handlung*]. Such an ordination would not, like the blessing of lay elders in the Prussian Church, be a purely human initiative, but could lay claim to the precedent [110] and indirect command of the apostles and to the whole of antiquity.

The Lutheran Church does not elevate ordination and the laying on of hands to the level of an absolutely necessary rite, while other churches, the Roman and the English [Anglican][21], deem it necessary. She does so because Holy Scripture lacks a universal command of the apostles to this effect. The present writer must nevertheless confess for his own person that he would have scruples of conscience about subordinating himself to a non-ordained presbyter. He cannot think to himself that what the apostles prescribed and held to for each rung [*Stufe*] of the office and for all congregations–a state of affairs that justifies itself and that, if it did not exist, would be desired–may be regarded as an indifferent human rite. *Ordaining in the name of the Triune God, if no command lies at hand, is a hazardous procedure.* In practice the Lutheran Church too has held to ordination, and her teaching concerning the grace of office shows that ordination can be much less a matter of indifference to her than seems to be the case when we hear and read that it is not commanded.

We have also already drawn attention in another place to the fact that the Lutheran Church does not repeat ordination, but even allows heretical ordination to stand. This practice makes no sense if ordination is nothing more than the solemn declaration of a call received. I ask again: should this be so, what then is installation as we have it? Why do we then refuse it the name of ordination? What interest do we have in calling a completely identical rite at a change of title[22] a new ordination? [111] Why do we separate the two? Here lies an inconsistency that cries out for resolution, that requires a different form of installation, and that brings to consciousness a higher view of ordination, which already lies within our souls. Ordination is *either* a ceremony of induction into particular spheres of official responsibility, in which case it can be repeated; *or* it cannot be repeated and is therefore more, the conferral of the presbyterate and its official authority in perpetuity, the separation and sanctification of the ordinand for the office, the impartation of authority to carry out the office wherever a particular call entails it.[14] Consider and pay heed to what you

14 The Lutheran dogmaticians know nothing of an ordination of *missionaries*. They speak against the Genevans, who sent missionaries into the Roman congregations of France. Missionaries have no title for which they might be ordained, no sphere of operation for which they might need authorization. Even so, at the present time missionaries are being ordained among Lutherans, without any objections being raised. It is *not* to be objected to if ordination is more than mere announcement of call received. It *is* to be objected to if it is no more than this. A plain testimony of the sore point of this locus [=dogmatics topic]! The reason the presbyterate ordains no one without a title is not that it confers its authority only for a single sphere of operation but simply so that everything may be done in good order. It can, however, impart its authority when it knows and

decide. To come down on the [112] second side will be to elevate the office, so that the man sanctified thereto not only has the call to inward sanctification, but the congregation has a call to hold the sanctified one sacred.

> Note. I have purposely not touched the most important passage Heb 6:2 on the ἐπίθεσις χειρῶν [laying on of hands].

---

trusts the man, because a missionary, a πρεσβύτερος περιοδεύτης, is needed, the grace of office to teach, authority to baptize, absolve, and commune those who have become believers. Free[ly operating] love [see endnote 10!], that preaches among unbelievers, finds a stop sign in the way of trust that it has actually received the office.

X. Remark on Teaching and Preaching without Ordination

37. Some passages, to which occasional reference has already been made in these sections, show us rather obviously that, according to the sense of the Bible, certain kinds of teaching without ordination are thinkable. Quite apart from the gift of prophecy, where the Holy Spirit did not bind Himself to offices, we find in Ac 8:4ff and 11:19ff that many non-ordained teachers worked among unbelieving Jews and Gentiles. We read in Ac 8:1 that after the death of St Stephen such a persecution arose against the congregation of Jerusalem that all except the apostles were scattered in the regions of Judea and Samaria (πάντες διεσπάρησαν κατὰ τὰς χώρας τῆς Ἰουδαίας καὶ Σαμαρείας πλὴν τῶν ἀποστόλων). And not only were they scattered, but they went around and preached the Gospel (οἱ μὲν οὖν διασπαρέντες διῆλθον εὐαγγελιζόμενοι τὸν λόγον [8:4]). In connection with this passage St Luke tells in Ac 11:19ff that those who were scattered after the persecution at Stephen's death came as far as Phoenicia, [113] Cyprus, and Antioch and told the Gospel to none but Jews. But some men from Cyprus and Cyrene came to Antioch, preached the Gospel also to Greeks, the hand of the Lord was with them, and a great company converted to Christ (Οἱ μὲν οὖν διασπαρέντες ἀπὸ τῆς θλίψεως τῆς γενομένης ἐπὶ Στεφάνῳ διῆλθον ἕως Φοινίκης καὶ Κύπρου καὶ Ἀντιοχείας μηδενὶ λαλοῦντες τὸν λόγον εἰ μὴ μόνον Ἰουδαίοις. Ἦσαν δέ τινες ἐξ αὐτῶν ἄνδρες Κύπριοι καὶ Κυρηναῖοι, οἵτινες ἐλθόντες εἰς Ἀντιόχειαν ἐλάλουν καὶ πρὸς τοὺς Ἑλληνιστὰς εὐαγγελιζόμενοι τὸν κύριον Ἰησοῦν καὶ ἦν χεὶρ κυρίου μετ' αὐτῶν, πολύς τε ἀριθμὸς ὁ πιστεύσας ἐπέστρεψεν ἐπὶ τὸν κύριον. [Ac 11:19-21]).

Now since this preaching is attributed to all who were scattered, but all who were scattered certainly did not stand in the teaching office, we shall surely have to admit that there was a preaching without office, which proceeded from an impulse of pure love, and which pleased the Lord so well that His hand was at work to produce a great catch of fish. And what is attributed to these layfolk and their like is not only the first needful work of necessity and love in the preaching office, not only the act of evangelization, but Ac 15:35 furnishes a passage from which we glimpse that also in the already established congregation of Antioch some who did not have the teaching office worked for the good of the Church [*Gemeine*]. It is said there of Paul and Barnabas that they stayed in Antioch and taught and preached *with many others* (Παῦλος δὲ καὶ Βαρναβᾶς διέτριβον ἐν Ἀντιοχείᾳ διδάσκοντες καὶ εὐαγγελιζόμενοι μετὰ καὶ ἑτέρων πολλῶν τὸν λόγον τοῦ κυρίου. [Ac 15:35]). [114] Notice not only ἕτεροι πολλοί ["with many others also" RSV] but also the attribution to them of εὐαγγελίζεσθαι in addition to διδάσκειν, i.e., of an activity toward the further formation of those already gathered.

These passages are very similar to what Eusebius says in the passage mentioned above concerning the "evangelists" who remained at the outset of the second century and concerning the zeal of many who went out and preached the Gospel under much blessing. Examples such as those of Aedesius and Frumentius also belong here.

It follows from all this that Luther and our dogmaticians after him are right when they say that, in case of necessity, in areas where no Gospel would be preached (or where wolves dominate) layfolk too would have the right and duty to preach. One can therefore issue no reproach when pious men of unblemished reputation, motivated by pure love, go among heathen, Jews, and degenerate Christians and preach Jesus to them from the yearning of their soul. We cannot deny that the hand and blessing of God are at work in such situations. Keeping this fact in our eye, we might draw many an important conclusion with respect to mission. Every Christian who lives among the heathen has hereby his marching orders, and every tongue should speak of the Lord's salvation and kingdom! Blessing can come upon the activity of each, and the one thing necessary is that everything take place in simplicity and humility.

[115]

XI. The First Synod at Jerusalem

§38.1. The great question of the Gentiles' sharing in the kingdom of God had to be thrown up at the crossing of the threshold from the Old to the New Testament, and this issue occasioned the first synod of the Christian Church. The Spirit of God had for this reason already led the first of the apostles, St Peter, into the truth, before decisions were taken in other places concerning the Gentiles' participation in Christ without the works of the Law, without circumcision etc. If this had not happened, it would at all events have been very hard for Jewish and Judaizing souls to acknowledge as of equal status with themselves and to relate in terms of brotherly love with Gentiles who had come to Christ without going through the transitional point of the Law. Even after these divine revelations had occurred, it was still intensely difficult for Jewish Christians to compose themselves and believe in a communion of saints established with pure Gentiles! Yet the spadework was done [in Peter's vision], and it could not be difficult for those who had received the revelation of the Holy Spirit for this issue to realize which side would emerge victorious when the decision was made.

2. In the great metropolis of the Gentile Christians, in Antioch, where believers from Cyprus and Cyrene (Ac 11:20) had called Gentiles with the sweet Gospel and led them to the Church [*Gemeine*], the struggle between Jewish and Gentile Christians burst out with vigor when Jewish Christians had come down from Jerusalem and insisted that Gentile Christians be circumcised. The prestige of Barnabas and [116] Paul was not sufficient to allay the storm. The congregation thereupon resolved to dispatch Paul and Barnabas and some others to Jerusalem to seek a decision there from the "*apostles and elders*" (Ἔταξαν ἀναβαίνειν Παῦλον καὶ Βαρναβᾶν καί τινας ἄλλους ἐξ αὐτῶν πρὸς τοὺς ἀποστόλους καὶ πρεσβυτέρους εἰς Ἰερουσαλὴμ, Ac 15:2).

Yet even in Jerusalem, where the revelation to St Peter and the conversion of Cornelius were well known, the issue aroused conflict and some Pharisees who had come to faith stiffly insisted on the circumcision of Gentile Christians. The apostles and elders then gathered to examine the issue (Συνήχθησάν τε οἱ ἀπόστολοι καὶ οἱ πρεσβύτεροι ἰδεῖν περὶ τοῦ λόγου τούτου., v. 6).

3. The gathering was not called for the apostles to gain a clear grasp of the issue for the first time. The *elders* will scarcely have been lacking light. The whole point of the exercise was for the benefit of the *congregations* at Jerusalem and Antioch and for the establishment of calm and peace between the conflicting parties. This is why the apostles and elders did not assemble privately, but gathered before the whole congregation in such a way that everyone could listen and also participate. The very expression "long debate" in vs. 7 (πολλὴ συζήτησις) hints at a gathering of many, while the presence of a large crowd emerges especially clearly from vss. 12, 22, and 23 respectively: "And *all the assembly* kept silence" [RSV] (Ἐσίγησεν πᾶν τὸ πλῆθος). "Then it seemed good to the apostles and the elders, *with the whole church*" [RSV] [117] (Ἔδοξε τοῖς ἀποστόλοις καὶ τοῖς πρεσβυτέροις σὺν ὅλῃ τῇ ἐκκλησίᾳ). "We, the apostles and elders and *brethren*" (Οἱ ἀπόστολοι καὶ οἱ πρεσβύτεροι καί οἱ ἀδελφοὶ).

4. It seems we must deduce the active participation of the congregation in the discussion from the πολλὴ συζζτησις, the "long debate," of vs. 7. And yet the actual decision is made by Peter (v. 7ff) and James (v. 13ff), the latter of whom in v. 19 uses in his concluding discourse the expression, "Therefore I judge" (Διὸ ἐγὼ κρίνω).[15] The Antiochenes had turned to the apostles and elders, and they are the ones who assembled to make up their minds. They have no secret, however. Nor were the congregational members present turned away, but were permitted to speak. This is made clear by the debate (συζήτησις) and by the

---

15 Cf. xvi:14, κεκριμένα

whole situation. Moreover, we must conclude from vs. 23 and 25 that the congregation was asked for its consent.

5. Given the right to understand each biblical passage in its full exactness, we might wish to press the expression in v. 24 τινὲς ἐξ ἡμῶν, "some persons from us" [RSV], from which it appears that the assembly in Jerusalem was separate and distinct from the other congregations and their assemblies and thus that this assembly was a kind of city or at most provincial synod. On this basis one might claim that the greatest caution should be employed when drawing conclusions from this assembly with respect to the synodical system in general. Gladly as we concede this point, though, we have a certain licence [118] to draw sure conclusions inasmuch as apostles were present at the assembly and led the first synod in a manner that is certainly worthy of all imitation. Nor do we find that the synod lacked prestige and decisive force, but read to the contrary in Ac 16:4[16] that its decisions were delivered by Paul and Timothy to all congregations in Asia Minor, and we can conclude that they were also universally received. Just as the congregation of Antioch heard the synodical letter with great joy in Ac 15:31, so all Gentile Christians everywhere can only have rejoiced as this document rendered them completely certain of their faith and practice.

6. In consequence of what has already been said, I should like to recommend that we apply the following inferences to the structuring of our synodical system:

I. *The core of a synod* is the presbytery, i.e., all the presbyters or elders present. They are the ones to whom the questions are posed, and they are the ones who assemble and make decisions as synod.

II. Synods are *public*, that is, no congregational member who wants to be present can be turned away. [119] Also everyone,

---

16 παρεδίδοσαν αὐτοῖς (to the brothers in Asia Minor) φυλάσσειν τὰ δόγματα τὰ κεκριμένα ὑπὸ τῶν ἀποστόλων καὶ πρεσβυτέρων τῶν ἐν Ἱεροσολύμοις. "They delivered to them for observance the decisions which had been reached by the apostles and elders who were at Jerusalem."

according to gift and zeal, must have the right–obviously according to the prevailing rules of order–to make motions and to join in the discussion, as was the case in Jerusalem.

III. Every Christian belonging to the synodical district can be present, but the congregations as such, as separate from and over against the presbyters, have *no representatives*.[17] [23] The shepherds represent the flock that they tend, and the flock trusts them to do so. Should there be representatives apart from against the presbytery, the Church would be conceived entirely according to the standpoint of the modern State, where the rulers are the constant objects of the distrust of the ruled and where the local communities [*Gemeinden*] adopt an attitude of mistrust to the rulers. This standpoint would only prove that neither flocks nor sheep are as they are meant to be. For all mistrust in the relationship between the two comes from the evil one; both must be able and willing to trust each other.

IV. *A congregation that does not belong to the district* can send a *deputation* to the synodical assembly, as did Antioch to Jerusalem. Indeed, such a deputation can summon a synodical assembly, [120] as we see in Jerusalem. No command is issued to such a deputation or congregation, but it is given advice (ἐξ ὧν διατηροῦντες ἑαυτοὺς εὖ πράξετε, Ac 15:29).

V. As in Jerusalem everybody's συζήτησις ["debate"] came before the apostles' instruction and the latter had the last word, so there are distinct advantages in letting the less mature and experienced speak first and having the most tried and tested speak last.

VI. Neither in Jerusalem nor elsewhere in the Church is there any regard for *majority vote*, but the simple counsel of apostles or elders is simply accepted, permeates the crowd, and is turned

---

17 We are speaking here against an *institutionalized* representation of the congregation over against the shepherds. Conversely, there may be good reasons for participating congregations to defend and exercise their right to be present at synods through congregational members whom they send, if they themselves are too distant to be present in goodly number.

by the apostles into a finished conclusion. The best word finds the best place, and this is how it should be.

VII. Synods do not have merely an advisory role toward the congregations, but they make decisions in the name of the congregation, and no single congregation may withdraw from [the synod's] decisions without leaving the diocese. Just look at the decisive force of the first church assembly and its δόγματα κεκριμένα.

We hope that these sentences will be as correct as they are simple, and comparisons with present conditions should not discourage us from watching and praying that we might more closely approximate to the apostolic prototype. God help us also in this point!

[121]

XII. Application of the Foregoing to the Present Circumstances

§39. 1. Hardly anything engages the friends of the Church right now as much as the question of her polity. And who would want to deny that it is high time to air this question? Unfortunately, we have all too often neglected to get ourselves a clear reply. Instead we have borne and plodded along with the status quo, even though we have suffered under it to an extraordinary degree.[24] Every eye that wants to see sees that the deficiencies and evils of the existing form of polity of the Protestant Church have depressed her fortunes to such an extent that in three hundred years the Lutheran Church has been unable to gain the form that would have won her respect from the outside and that would have rendered her fit to be for the world what her birth from the word of God and the Church's call to blessing required her to be. Living in marriage with the State, the Church has not been happy; her landlord ruled; she could not think of a free unfolding of her glory, of a development of her life and essence. It is indeed correct that the landlord was sometimes in a good mood and allowed a little elbowroom for the sake of his domestic honor. We can be thankful to him that he did not behave even worse than he did. But what is true remains true, and on the whole the connection between State and Church has been an unhappy mismatch.

2. Now it is coming apart. What God did not join together [122] is going asunder–and now everyone wants to help the Church through polity. And yet the evil lies much deeper. The Church's decay did not come in first place from her form and external arrangement, however much this helped to bring her to the depths in which we now behold her. The evil will therefore not be lifted through a mere change of polity. By the wrath of God the Word itself was lost to clergy and people for decades on end. Where it

began to be heard again there was a lack of understanding and care for pure doctrine and for the gift of distinguishing the spirits. What sounded Christian was taken for Christian, and at the time when the first love was again awoken a strict division of true from false was deemed lovelessness. Thus folk preached, taught, and confessed all manner of things, different and contrary things, and people rejoiced when an injudicious love felt authorized to bear with every point of view, to find and openhandedly concede truth in everything. At an earlier stage syncretism had been the twilight leading into the evil night of unbelief, and now syncretism became the dawn leading into a new day. The same open-handed permissiveness toward opinions begot a tolerance of all kinds of lifestyles, a syncretism of life. People mutually dispensed forgiveness when they lived worldly lives according to a generally Christian viewpoint; they mutually indulged the darkness within. Their wading into the river of justification through faith alone was too shallow for them to emerge purified in minds, thoughts, and desires. Cowardly flirtation was no love. The Church turned into a chaos of opinions at odds with each other [123] and into an undisciplined mob with the clergy by and large as a band of dumb dogs wagging their tails. Far be it from us to rebuke those who deserve no censure. Praise God there were and are exceptions who are worthy of all honor. But was not the situation by and large as I have described? And is it not for the most part still the same? And can polity alone help such a decayed flock? She must repentantly return to the point from which she fell. If she does not do this, let her polity be whatever people want: the Lord is emphatically not present. To the pure word and confession without separating what God has joined! Let us not pick and choose according to our whims, but return at the same time to discipline and serious Christian living. Polity will then help us forward. A man sick unto death does not get better just by being clad in a glorious garment. When he is healthy, he helps to dress himself and instinctively reaches for the best clothing.

3. In the meantime, since everyone is talking about polity, permit us to join in the discussion and, even though we do not fall in with the opinion of many others, allow us honestly to put in our two cents' worth. We too would go straight to the issue that causes so much misery and annoyance, the thing that we cannot hold on to and yet do not know how to detach ourselves from: we mean the princes' role as "supreme bishops." Time brought this into being, and now time is taking it away again. It provoked tears enough while it was up and running, and we should let it take its leave without complaint. We emphatically do not wish to speak of Roman Catholic princes' exercising the role of "supreme bishop" over Protestant churches: the contradiction involved in this state of affairs is its own judge, and folk should long since have been ashamed to defend a "supreme episcopate" of this kind. [124] But what else is even the "supreme episcopate" of a prince of the same religion than the monstrous offspring of the territorial system? Where did the Church ever *confer* on the princes anything of the kind claimed by the jurists? What do the princes have in this matter that they did not snatch or that their secular authority did not at any rate draw to itself, unconsciously yet irresistibly, as the magnet draws iron? But if the principle *cuius regio, eius religio* ["of whom the territory, of him the religion"][25] is now history, if the territorial system is sinking, and if the States are now bidding adieu to religion, what does anyone want with the supreme episcopacy of the princes? If the prince of a constitutional State wants to continue as supreme bishop of a church, will the spirit of the age permit him to exempt this side of his activity from the counter-signature of his ministers and to devote himself to the Church? Certainly not! The State fears the Church and wants guarantees that the prince will not be influenced, especially not by the Church. Hence, to use the expression a second time, the [government] minister must give his counter-signature to the prince's episcopate and to all his pronouncements in its regard. In a case where the prince himself is pious but the minister and the legislature to which he is responsible are unfavorable to the

Church, what guarantees does the Church then have that she will not be influenced, pressured, and enslaved as dreadfully as ever happened in the past? What then is the supreme episcopate of a constitutional prince? Why do we not simply drop it along with everything connected with it and everything that no longer makes sense when the territorial ruler is no longer in fact the *episcopus*? What is a territorial Church in the prevailing sense when the territorial ruler is no longer *episcopus*? The periphery [125] disappears with the center. And what are consistories when there is no longer a bishop? After all, where there is no center, there are no radii. All of this hangs together. As the spirit of the age casts down the one, so it casts down the other. Anyone who seeks to salvage the one or the other clings to ruins that will all collapse in their time. The system no longer holds together. But we see in its fate what is bound up with the episcopal name and we understand why so many are clinging for dear life to the princely supreme episcopate: they see sheer ruin in the offing. And they are right to do so–albeit in a way that merits reproach–for their faith has lost sight of the word that the Church rests upon a rock and that the gates of hell shall not overwhelm her. In comparison with this nothing stands or falls with the princely supreme episcopate, with which much else can tumble, even much that happens to be useful, and yet which is nothing that cannot be restored a hundredfold.

4. Yet might not the entire previous structure be preserved, even if the princely supreme episcopate collapses? Might not the formerly royal governing body afterwards become a churchly governing body, that is, one that proceeds from the Church herself? We do not hide the fact that in the end of the day the Church will still remain in a certain connection with the State, that there will be much to do in this respect. Yet once we get beyond the transitional stage there might be a considerable diminution of the tasks that went hand in hand with the former arrangements. Where the connection of State and Church has ceased over a longer period, we can at least make this remark: there will be less governing and [126] writing to do for the simple reason that more

rights will flow to the individual congregation that can then be exercised more economically. In such a situation we might be saddled with much less work and governing, so that a number of workers and business people might be dismissed and the Church spared much money. There is always much thought of the Church's polity being democratically based, and it is also probable that a system of majority voting will implement just such a system. But how should a supreme governing body, like a supreme consistory or even just a consistory, agree with democracy? In that case such a governing body is completely superfluous, and all the more so should we decide for a synodal-presbyteral system. The general synod decides for wider, the synod for narrower circles; the synods implement the decisions of the general synod, and the presbyteries those of the synods. And if some person or congregation has no desire to implement some resolution or other, who will compel them to do so once everything is free? What point would there be in consistories and supreme consistories if a synodal-presbyteral system is consistently implemented? We could refer to the Lutheran Church of Prussia, which is headed by a supreme ecclesiastical council [*Oberkirchenkollegium*], but the synodical system has not been implemented there energetically enough to support this structure. Conversely, we can refer to the North American setup, which has sprouted from the spirit of the age, for which reason it must appear to many as more normative. A council at a church's head indicates an unfinished building. In this case a church's polity is to be compared with a broken-off top pillar, and it is at [127] all events incomprehensible what independent position it is supposed to occupy if supreme authority lies in the hands of the synod (general synod). In the end of the day it remains the case that a consistory is the supreme council of a bishop and without him it would at least have a completely different position. It will make a poor showing as surrogate of a bishop. We might indeed say that even when a synodical system is implemented a standing governing body will be necessary for the time during which there is no synod. Yet the Americans delegate to their synodical president sufficient authority to accomplish all tasks that arise between their synodical assemblies and they assign him the duty of calling an extraordinary synodical assembly in important cases. This device caters for all urgent contingencies and extraordinary synods are only very seldom necessary beyond the regular yearly synods. It is also natural: the simplest arrangement is in keeping with democratic foundations. Cheap as it is, such an arrangement suffers little and causes little suffering in the vicissitudes of synodical life and with the frequent ebb and flow of participants at synodical gatherings.

5. As is shown by what follows, we have not said this from personal partisanship for a synodal-presbyteral system. We have simply gone with the flow of what we commonly hear said in our days. We see embarrassment on almost every side. Recourse upwards, to the princes, is no longer a viable option. A purely democratic foundation? That is not viable either. A participation of the people in churchly matters is here presupposed that does not at all exist and that, if it [128] did exist, would be all the more dangerous because a participation without confessional faithfulness and discipline can only have a corrupting effect. Just look at the secular members of our diocesan synods if you want to perceive both of these factors. They are either speechless yes men or they gang up against the clergy. Such alien elements can only have the hindering effects of a ball and chain. Obviously, there are exceptions to this rule. The reason for all this embarrassment is a reluctance to begin at the right place. The Church is corrupt precisely because the world has infiltrated her and gained possession. It does not help to say that the Church is an educator of humanity. She is and should be this, but she is not nor can she be this, if she herself is secularized. We cannot seriously say that her heavenly call as educator involves receiving hordes of children of the world into her bosom and membership simply in order to have many to educate! The Church is nothing for humanity, or at any rate not as much as she should be if, lacerated and secularized in herself, she does not possess the divine powers and the virtues

necessary to have an effect on others. In order to bear with such a host of worldly people–we do not say with "hypocrites and Christians with their mouths only"–without ourselves being crushed by them, we would have to join the Roman Church which is renowned for having found the means to cope with this burden. In order to find a church polity, we must first have a *Church*, i.e., people who, even though there are hypocrites among them, nevertheless deem themselves bound to the confession and to obedience [129] to God's word, and who can generally be credited with a Christian disposition. If we have such people, then there is no difficulty with congregations sharing in the governance of the Church. For such people become acquainted from Holy Scripture with the limits of their participation and conceive respect for the holy office to which, according to God's Word, belongs first place in the governance of the Church. This is how it is: *everything depends on acknowledgment of the holy office, of its relationship to the congregation, and of the congregation's relationship to it.* This perception is absolutely foundational in matters of polity. But even though this is true, one is not permitted to say so. People's ears are hostile to such talk. For the office must be nothing, and some of those who hold it have such a low opinion of it that they themselves put it down and help to drag it through the dust. Yet what is a bishop but an overseer over the Church of Christ, a shepherd? And what is a shepherd supposed to do? Simply tend the sheep, yet without guiding, leading, or governing them, so long as what he does is poles removed from ruling? But let right remain what it is, namely, right, and recognize bishops as those rightfully invested with the governance of the Church, as presbyters, elders. For "bishop" is a name derived from the calling, "presbyter" from the dignity proper to it, and yet one and the same person and office is described by both names.

6. The relationship of office to congregation is seldom rightly perceived and yet more seldom rightly ordered. In the Roman Communion and in the other churchly communions whose polities are similar to hers, [130] the people, the congregation, recedes too

much behind the office and its holders. In our Protestant churches of Germany the prince formerly pushed back both people and office. In North America the congregation predominates in an unseemly fashion. Even our sister congregations in Prussia may not have weighed completely correctly what belongs to the office and what to the congregation. In this context we concede that in the end of the day we find an over-mighty prince more bearable than an over-mighty congregation. To the extent that it influenced the Church, the division of the congregation into the three estates [*Lehr-, Wehr-, und Nährstand*] is a kind of human figment to whose defense such glorious men as our older theologians ought never to have lent themselves. In the congregation the prince belongs quite simply to the people, and there is no division beyond that between office and people. But if one of the people had to rule, it was always better for the prince to rule than, as at present, for all members of the congregation to rule and to want to run things according to majority rule in the house of God, where God's word and wisdom should be what counts. If tyranny there must be, one tyrant is more bearable than many. There is so much talk about the people's maturity in political things and there is a desire to transfer this maturity to the sphere of spiritual things. And yet a maturity that would decide in churchly things freely and according to majority vote is absolutely nowhere attributed even to the *pious* people. Even the first congregations were not mature in this sense, for they all stood under the office. [131] Maturity must be understood in different terms, given that we learn in Gal 4:1-7 that the underage son exercises the obedience of the strict school, the mature son that of the free, insightful will. Both honor the father's command, but each in a different way, from a different spiritual foundation. Should the people be mature, it will not *want* to rule, but rather desire to be led according to God's word, and it will judge and acknowledge such leading with a mature mind.

7. The relationship between office and congregation that we find in the New Testament, in the Acts of the Apostles, and in the Epistles is very simple, entirely scriptural, and at the same time

entirely in keeping with the kernel of truth that lies in the demands of our time. There lurks in this relationship at once something *aristocratic* and something *democratic*, something constant and something in a state of flux. Neither in State nor in Church should we completely shun an aristocratic element. In neither the realm of nature nor the realm of grace is there complete equality, but one finds everywhere a great and a small, an above and a beneath. In the absence of great and small, there is no charm; in the absence of above and beneath, no order. As certainly as God is a God of order and His Spirit a Spirit who charmingly distinguishes and unites great and small etc., so must there also be an aristocratic element in Church as well as State. Yet there must also be something democratic, because without a lively participation of the congregation there is no lively Church, and without freedom there is no lively participation. The aristocratic element lies in the *presbyterate*, the democratic in the *diaconate*. [132] The first congregation built herself through these two offices. She propagated both with herself, as we have read. Congregations would have to build themselves through both again today, if they would make provision for the whole life and love of Christians.

8. We are speaking here, by the way, just as little of *lay* elders as of *secular* welfare workers. Both offices are holy and their holders are ordained. We have already said that the name appropriate to the calling of elders or presbyters is *"bishop, overseer."* To this office of overseeing and shepherding belongs everything that God founded, ordered, and implied in the means of grace and so-called *subsidia* of salvation. It is an office "of prayer and the word," of liturgy and sacrament, of preaching, teaching, pastoral care, discipline, and order. We indeed find in Holy Scripture a distinction between teachers and elders. The teacher can be an elder, but does not have to be; he can (as in our case, e.g., university professors of theology) teach without standing in the holy office. Conversely, the elder does not have to be a teacher, but he can be, and the apostle does demand a certain amount of "aptitude to teach" of all elders. For our epoch this remark implies

that the presbyterate is not dependent in the first instance on the gifts that a teacher must have. Neither first-rate talent for teaching nor first-rate training for the teaching office is necessary for the presbyterate. There must at all times be "teachers," scholars, theologians in the Church, yet it is a one-sided development for which church history—especially that of our own day—has paid a high price [133] when *only* teachers, scholars, theologians have been entrusted with the presbyterate. This procedure has stood on its head the initial position of the office of elder. To begin with, elders were taken from the congregations themselves, and first-rate teachers came and were called from afar. Now it only happens by accident that an elder comes from a congregation over which he is to preside. Mostly congregations receive strangers of whom they can give no testimony and exercise no judgment. It thus comes about quite naturally that congregations cannot actively participate in the election of elders, to the extent that this is guaranteed them in Holy Scripture, or that they can only do so in the most superficial way. All popular participation in this election simply goes down the drain. So-called patronage of congregations, where it exists, is something quite different from a congregational participation in the election of elders in keeping with Scripture. The most important point is that, because elders no longer emerge from the congregation, we suffer a dearth of the most powerful organ of influencing the congregation, because the rector [*Pfarrer*], who is almost more teacher than he is elder, lacks the trust, the knowledge, and the whole position enjoyed by those elders. We pick up a sense of this state of affairs when it is suggested that we adopt lay elders, secular presbyteries. But more often than not these lay elders oppose the rector [*Pfarrer*] or do not stand in right relationship to him. Everything would be different if there were ordained elders from the congregations into whose midst an elder with university training could still step. According to the measure of their gift those ordained elders could do and look after everything just the same as the elder with university training. The one with university training, though, [134] the elder and teacher of the congregation, would stand among the elders as *primus inter pares* [first among equals] and, while on terms of complete equality with them, would still stand over them in virtue of his knowledge and prevent error and false doctrine from gaining entrance into the college of elders. Such ordained elders from the congregation would at the same time become a new means of educating the congregation. The requirements that should feature in the examination according to the First Epistle to Timothy and that to Titus demand preparation and diligence in sanctification on the part of the candidate, and the delight in the holy office that might be aroused in the congregations would motivate men all the more strongly to pursue the appropriate formation. At the same time there would arise within the college of elders a sacred duty for its successors and their formation. There would be acolytes or disciples who, as they kept company with the elders and received their instruction, would ripen for the holy office in the most natural soil and grow in the house of God for the discharge of its affairs. What we have said sounds whimsical. But what would prevent us, as new congregations arise, from introducing the most tried and tested mechanism of Holy Scripture, which antiquity and later on the Bohemian Brethren followed in their church order? Newly emerging congregations that gathered on the basis of the confession and the command of Jesus would right at the outset have the manpower that our present congregations offer only sparingly.

9. With regard to the *election* of elders, this will ensue through the existing elders themselves in consultation with the congregation. Should an elder die or move permanently [135] to another place, the presbyterate propagates itself. If new congregations arise, which as yet have no presbyterate, the necessary number of elders is appointed for them in consultation with the congregational members either by the presbyterate of the neighboring localities or by one charged with this duty by his brethren and fellow elders (the bishop of the diocese). Such a procedure follows from the apostolic passages and from the circumstance that presbyteries

ordained presbyters (Timothy in Lystra) and that presbyters ordained and appointed presbyteries (Titus in Crete, Timothy in Ephesus). As we apply these prototypes to the context of our own times, we should not forget that congregational participation in the election of presbyters ought not in general to be stretched too far. Much less ought we to hand over the whole process of election to congregations in their present condition. There is no need to demonstrate at length to what great dangers to salvation those congregations would be exposed who do not enjoy any leading and moderating influence as they go about the business of electing presbyters.

10. Things stand quite otherwise with the *deacons*. They are the welfare officers of the congregations, those to whom the treasures of the congregation, her funds for poor relief, her poor box, are entrusted for this and related purposes (such as remuneration of "teachers," the upkeep of church buildings, attention to the Church's practical needs). They are freely elected by the congregation according to the apostolic norm, they are approved and ordained by the presbytery, stand under the presbytery and its supervision, and form a rung geared toward the presbyterate. They exercise indeed no power of the keys, they cannot intrude into the presbyterate, the "office of prayer and the word" stands [136] as a distinct entity above them. But everything that can appear important to the congregation beyond the dominically instituted office and its sphere of operation, that is, its poor, its alms and oblations, lies in the hands of the deacons. The congregation elects these officers freely, without any participation by the presbytery; it can therefore commit its gifts and its resources for the relief of the poor entirely to men it trusts. Since the deacons enjoy its trust, the congregation will not mistrust them; and since they are subordinates enjoying its blessing, they will not act against the supervising presbytery. Thus they occupy a rightful middle place between presbytery and congregation, loved and respected by both, and each Christian rejoices in the beautiful order. As they proceed from the midst of the congregations, the two offices fulfil all the

reasonable desires of the congregation itself, and through the two it is possible to meet fully all the needs of the congregations, both spiritual and material.

11. Just as both offices have emerged from the election and midst of the congregation, the one according to its nature more than the other, so the two never stand without the congregation. They rule and order all the congregation's concerns. But in the event that new cases arise that have not yet been discussed, that fall outside the authority of the presbytery, or that the congregation does not understand without instruction, the presbytery assembles the "whole company" (πᾶν πλῆθος) of the disciples. While the *congregational assembly* is not the final authority, it is nevertheless briskly involved in all things undertaken by presbyters and deacons, even in matters of governance. Its participation [137] ensures that the good will of the "whole company" remains healthy and strong and causes all to register the fact that they are not lorded-over but governed aright.

12. Congregations that are organized in this way stand on the same foundation of faith and life, and have the same administration of the sacraments, feel themselves related and attracted to one another. The word and sacrament of the Lord join them as members into a single whole, a single body. The Lord wills that as members they cleave together in love. They thus seek connection, a connection rendered easier by their having the same needs. To the extent that they know each other and to the extent that it is feasible, they form a single congregation. Their presbyters together are a single presbyterate, their deacons a single diaconate. Just as in the presbytery of the single congregations the διδάσκαλος, the "teacher" or another significant man, emerges automatically above his peers to be acknowledged as their chief [*Vorsteher*], so in virtue of the same syndrome on the territory of an entire presbytery or diocese, whether by acclamation or by election, a presiding officer [*Präses*], visitor [*Visitator*], ordinator, a bishop, a pastor [*Seelsorger*] elected by all for all, likewise automatically arises to watch over common concerns and to deal with current

business. And just as a presiding officer arises over the presbyters, so likewise an archdeacon arises over the deacons. Furthermore, just as the most important cases of communal concern in the individual congregations would come before the congregational assembly, so likewise an assembly of bishops and deacons and of all Christians of the diocese who are able and willing to take part can discuss the common concerns of the diocese. [138] And just as the presbytery rendered the final decision in the individual congregational assembly, so likewise in the diocesan assembly. Not majority vote, but God's Word is victorious. In matters of less moment, temporal matters, the opinion that makes headway can carry the day–here, then, a kind of majority vote. Deputies *can* be sent by the congregations, yet without excluding the free participation of other congregational members, and not standing corporately [as a *corpus*] over against the presbytery. *The image of the individual congregation repeats itself on the larger terrain of the diocese*: presbyterate, diaconate, each with its summit, with bishop and archdeacon; congregational assembly made up of presbyters, deacons, and free or deputized participants from the people. Everywhere aristocratic and democratic elements, everywhere a mature people that gladly lets itself be taught and directed. In this way a plurality of distinct dioceses can be formed. What joins them all is declared *church fellowship*, common faith, common obedience to God's Word, common discipline, the same offices (episcopate, presbyterate, diaconate), mutual recognition of ordination and excommunication and also, when it seems necessary, coming together for a council.

13. Over individuals and their [private] judgment stands the fellowship of the presbytery and the other brethren, the synod, the council. The individual presbyter, even the angel or bishop of the congregation, must let himself be directed and spoken to. Every dignitary can be suspended by decree of the synod, in settled cases [139] by the presbytery or the bishop. At the opening of the synod, a senior member asks whether there is any complaint against the bishop, and only after he has been declared irreproachable does

he take his seat as leader of the synod. He then asks whether there is any complaint against some presbyter, deacon, or brother. Only the irreproachable may take their seats and speak. This procedure, to which Holy Scripture offers no contradiction, would avert possible infringements by officeholders. Non-recognition of a decision of the synod would have as its consequence the voluntary or synodically enforced separation of the resisting member.

14. The outlines given above of a scriptural ordering of the relationship between office and congregation are certainly simple. They are also in keeping with nature and experience, and a long history of the Christian Church speaks for them. They unite the possibility of free movement, on the one hand, with constancy, firm order, and strength, on the other, and at the same time the whole guarantees one thing that is necessary for the purity of the Church, to the extent that it should be striven for, namely, ease of separating. A major point to emphasise in this time is that the proposals here advocated somehow transfigure the ideas of the age.[26] Admittedly, all of this will be nothing for churchly communions that consist for the most part in decayed masses of people that folk lack the courage, in obedience to Christ, either to exclude or to leave. Anyone who wants to hold together at any cost the de facto structure, be it as it will and whether the Lord's commands bid us leave it or put it aside, will find no taste for these aphorisms, which are written from a deep longing for better conditions and do not shrink [140] from the woes that must ensue if a Church worthy of the name should arise upon the old confession, a Church that is not, as was the case in the past, mostly the opposite of what she is meant to be. The Lord help His poor Church and grant His servants wisdom, courage, humility, strength, and steadfastness! Amen.

Editorial Endnotes

1 In light of the revolutions that swept through most of the 39 States of the German Confederation in the year 1848 and whose reverberations were still being keenly felt as these *Aphorisms* went to press, the reader might expect the translation to read "On the Question of the Church's *Constitution*." But whereas the German people were set on wringing constitutions out of their reluctant rulers in order to ensure a measure of elected participation in government, Löhe's concern was not to secure the sort of foundational written documents that feature so prominently in American church life, but rather with the role of the holy office in the actual governance of the Church. In an email to the translator, Professor Roland Ziegler of the Fort Wayne seminary agreed with his decision to translate *Verfassung* with "polity."

2 Johannes Deinzer, *Wilhelm Löhe's Leben: Aus seinem schriftlichen Nachlaß zusammengestellt*. I (2nd ed.) Nürnberg: Verlag von Gottfr. Löhe, 1874. II Gütersloh: Druck und Verlag von E. Bertelsmann, 1880. III Druck und Verlag von E. Berthelsmann, 1892. A portrait of Deinzer is found in Erika Geiger, *Wilhelm Löhe 1808-1872: Leben—Werk—Wirkung* (Nuendettelsau: Freimund Verlag, 2003), 314. Geiger, daughter of the late Landesbischof Hermann Dietzfelbinger, offers a biography that is at once scholarly and informative and pitched at a (relatively) popular level.

3 See Thomas M. Winger, "The Relationship of Wilhelm Löhe to C. F. W. Walther and the Missouri Synod in the Debate concerning Church and Office," *Lutheran Theological Review* VII: 1 &2:106-131. To access little known yet significant facts about Walther and early Missouri, see Jonathan F. Grothe, "Deposal and/or Removal: Principles, Practices, and Proposals," *Lutheran Theological Review* VII: 1 & 2:9-27.

4 All occurrences of the first person singular in the Foreword are in the third person singular in the original.

5 Lit. "according to the classification titles of ecclesiastical archeology"!

6 The original name of the church body usually known as Congregationalists.

7 Probably the pastoral conference held in the Neuendettelsau parsonage from 27 to 28 March 1848, as Löhe and some brethren in office pondered how to steer the turmoil of the 1848 Revolutions to the benefit of the Church. See D II:250-259.

8 Surely Löhe himself, who wrote in the sixth point of his summary of the meeting that, "the rebuilding of the Church should not start with blueprints of polity in general, but with a better shaping of congregations, of individual congregations from whose amalgamation and harmony a Church arises" (D II:255).

9 Feminine form in the original, reflecting Löhe's recognition of the feminine essence of the Church.

10 Löhe appears to be referring to Eusebius' *History of the Church* iii, 37, which, however, speaks of "many …belonging to the first stage in the apostolic succession," and thus almost certainly of clergy rather than laity.

11 Since the 1960s Löhe's "preaching free love" would be met with a smirk and hence needs paraphrase.

12 The definite article "das" is missing in the original, which has a space here.

13 In fact, book three.

14 "enan" in the original is obviously a misprint for "genannt."

15 Löhe says 1 Tim 5:17, but quotes 1 The 5:12.

16 Presumably the noun beginning E and continuing blank reads "Einen" (one)?

17 Löhe seems unaware of 1 Clement 44.

18 I render in italicized Greek print three words that Löhe emphasizes by placing them in *Sperrdruck* (spaced type).

19 Löhe's emphasis in original, as in 18.

20 "Thing to be devoutly desired," an allusion to the title of Spener's famous work, *Pia Desideria*.

21 Löhe is writing just sixteen years after John Henry Newman, in the first of the *Tracts for the Times*, articulated the modern high Anglican understanding of the threefold ministry, access to which could be gained only through a bishop standing in apostolic succession.

22 The ancient Church's term for our "call."

23 Although Löhe opposed the establishment of the office of *Vorsteher* (church council member?) that was introduced in the aftermath of the General Synod of 1849, he was pleasantly surprised to find the "church council" that was accordingly elected in Neuendettelsau a thoroughly cooperative body.

24 Other leading figures in the Neo-Lutheran movement saw things differently. At the Leipzig conference of August 1848, Theodor Kliefoth, superintendent in Mecklenburg, advocated the (albeit "nominal") continuance of a "reasonable" form of the princely "supreme episcopate" (D II: 278).

25 The principle underlying the "Religious Peace of Augsburg" of 1555.

26 Just as the "spirit of 1848" pushed for the introduction of constitutional monarchy in the political sphere, Löhe hoped that the royally appointed consistory that had ridden roughshod over clergy and laity would make way for a polity with appropriate involvement of what Lutheran Orthodoxy conceived as the two components of the *ecclesia synthetica* ("composite Church"), i.e., clergy and laity.

www.ingramcontent.com/pod-product-compliance
Lightning Source LLC
LaVergne TN
LVHW051841080426
835512LV00018B/3010